ACTIVE
PRAYER
SERIES

D0702138

Knit One, Purl a *prayer*

A Spirituality of Knitting   Peggy Rosenthal

PARACLETE PRESS
BREWSTER, MASSACHUSETTS

Knit One, Purl a Prayer: A Spirituality of Knitting

Copyright © 2011 by Peggy Rosenthal
ISBN 978-1-55725-806-9

Library of Congress Cataloging-in-Publication Data
Rosenthal, Peggy.
  Knit one, purl a prayer : a spirituality of knitting / Peggy Rosenthal.
    p. cm.
  Includes bibliographical references (p.   ).
  ISBN 978-1-55725-806-9 (p)
  1. Knitters (Persons)—Religious life. 2. Prayer—Christianity I. Title.
  BV4596.N44R67 2011

  248.8'8—dc23   2011032026

10 9 8 7 6 5 4 3 2 1

Published by Paraclete Press
Brewster, Massachusetts
www.paracletepress.com

Printed in the United States of America

3 1232 00968 7320

To *Amelia Templar,*
owner of Yarn Boutique in Rochester, New York,

and *Lynn Davis,*
owner of Kiwi Knitting Company in Tucson, Arizona:

Creators of Community

Contents

Preface

When I decided to learn to knit a few years ago, I thought I was learning so that I could teach the craft to my granddaughters, then ages six and eight. Little did I know what an enrichment knitting would become for my own life: how it would help me in sickness and in health, in times of tranquility and times of stress—how knitting would become a means of prayer.

I won't pretend that knitting was prayerful at first. Quite the contrary. Learning any new craft takes an attention that is all-absorbing; teaching one's brain to adapt to new movements of the body doesn't leave much space for the spirit to breathe freely. But over the months, as my hands began to move more comfortably through the stitches, my mind began to experience a spirit-filled presence. I didn't think of this as prayer until one day when I bumped into a friend at a lecture where I'd brought my knitting.

The story of how her offhand comment about knitting in prayerful silence utterly transformed my activity of knitting into one of prayer is told in chapter 1. For now, I'll just say that her comment moved me to experience the formation of each new stitch as something like praying with prayer beads.

Like praying with beads, yes; but also more. Because something tangible was being created as the yarn passed through my fingers: I was knitting the yarn into a visibly pleasing pattern as I prayed. This creativity, I came to realize as I pondered it over the months that followed, added a special dimension to my sense of Divine Presence as

I knit. In the Bible, we first meet God as the Creator. "In the beginning," the Bible opens, "God created the heavens and the earth." God goes on to create the light, the water, the land, all trees and plants, all animals and birds. Then God creates humankind—"in his image" (Gen. 1:26–27). Humankind is created in the image of the Creator.

Since we are created in the image of our Creator, it follows that we humans are created to create! Creativity is our calling. We can enact this creativity through any of the arts or crafts, as well as through what we might name the "art of living": engaging creatively in our world to join in the divine work to make it "good." Knitting partakes of this divinely ordained creativity.

So do all the creative arts. I come to the writing of this book after years of writing about how poetry can enhance our relationship to the Divine. Among my previous books are a study of how the figure of Jesus has been treated by contemporary poets of various cultures; an anthology of worldwide poems inspired by particular passages of the Gospels; and some reflection guides on how poetry can be a vehicle for prayer.

What has excited me in writing this current book on the spirituality of knitting is that, while both poetry and knitting are creative endeavors, knitting—unlike poetry—engages the mind and spirit through the work of our hands. Other crafts of course do this as well, but knitting is the work that my own hands love to do.

And I'm far from alone in this love. Knitting has entered a boom in popularity all around the world (an Indonesian Internet knitting site, for instance, is visited by people from Malaysia, Singapore, Japan, the Middle East, Holland, Germany, and the United States). South American countries such as Uruguay and Peru have been growing their economies through global exports of fine wool and yarn produced by local sheep and alpaca farmers, often working through cooperatives. Current knitters, mostly but not all women, range in age from grade school to grandmothers and cover every occupation. There are many sociological and psychological reasons for the current knitting craze. But one reason, I propose, is that knitting engages our creative spirits in a world where technology and corporate consumerism seem to have everything already done for us. Computers, cell phones, shopping malls, worldwide chain stores, and brand-name products can all be immensely useful; but they don't engage our spirit and can even stifle it. Knitters everywhere are discovering gratefully that knitting nurtures the spirit.

One doesn't have to be a knitter to read this book. I expect that it will be of most interest to knitters, but anyone who does handcrafts or has even considered doing them will find food for thought—and nourishment for the spirit, I hope, as well. For knitters, a pattern is offered at the end of each chapter of the book, fitted to the chapter's theme.

Only through inner peace can the spirit thrive. "Be still, and know that I am God," Psalm 46 quietly exhorts us. After a quarter-century of daily contemplative prayer practice—during which jumpy distractions and mental dartings here and there have been my main experience—I find that nothing brings me to inner stillness as knitting does. In our stillness, through our stillness, the Transcendent can become known to us.

This is a spiritual truth echoed in all major religious traditions—as I've come to learn gradually in the course of my life. I grew up in a household of Jewish ancestry, and although my parents did not belong to a synagogue and had relinquished most Jewish practices, I loved going to the synagogue with friends on the High Holy Days. Then, as a teenager, I wandered into a Cokesbury bookstore. I had no idea that this was a Christian store, but somehow I was moved to buy a "red-letter" Bible: one with all of Jesus' words printed in red. I'd browse in this Bible—the only one in my home—on Sundays, a day that had come to feel restless to me. I sensed I should be doing something special on Sundays but didn't know what. My neighborhood and high school were almost entirely Jewish, and I had no friends who went to church.

As a young adult, I was drawn, along with my husband, to baptism in the Catholic Church. A marvelous and unexpected result of becoming a Christian was that suddenly I was eager to learn about other faith traditions—Buddhism, Hinduism, Islam. So in this book, although my own spiritual grounding is Christian, I naturally draw on the spiritualities of other religions as well.

There is also another sort of outreach that has come naturally for this book: outreach to community, which is a key dimension of knitting. Knitters often create in order to give their work away to those in need; and knitters seek out one another for a unique sort of bonding. Knitting's communal dimension will be the specific topic of chapter 3, but I've tried to enact its spirit throughout the book—by giving voice to many other knitters besides myself. The spirituality of knitting is not a me-spirituality; rather, knitting draws us together. So I've folded into the book the experiences and insights of a multitude of knitters: some known to me personally, some the friends of friends, some whom I know only through their blogs or knitting websites. My thanks go out to all these people for sharing their perceptions and stories with me.

In the swing era of World War II, Glenn Miller had a hit song called "Knit One, Purl Two." The song's speaker is a woman knitting for her husband who is fighting in the war overseas:

Knit one, purl two
This sweater, my darling,'s for you
While vigil you're keeping through rain and storm
This sweater will keep you warm.

I wouldn't claim that the "vigil" here has a spiritual connotation, but I've borrowed the song's famous first line as my book's title. The line has been played with often: Knit One, Purl Too is the name of several knitting shops around the country; a recent mystery novel is titled *Knit One, Kill Two;* there's a knitting blog called *Knit Once, Purl Forever.* In this spirit of play, along with a spirit of exploratory adventure, I invite readers to *Knit One, Purl a Prayer.*

ONE

Knit One, Purl a Prayer

> When we knit, we place our attention
> over and over again on the natural
> rhythm of creating fabric from yarn.
> —Tara Jon Manning, *Mindful Knitting*

Praying with Your Fingers

I had been knitting for about a year and had gotten pretty comfortable with the basics. So, following the advice of my more experienced knitter friends, I began to take my knitting everywhere. One Sunday afternoon at a lecture hall, while I was sitting and knitting as I waited for the speaker to arrive, my friend Amanda passed by on the way to her seat. She stopped to chat and was looking at my knitting, so I asked, "Do you knit, too?" "Just prayer shawls," she said, shrugging.

I'd heard of prayer shawls but hadn't a clue what they were, so I seized the opportunity.

"What *are* prayer shawls?"

"You sit silently in a group," Amanda explained, "and everyone knits while praying."

I smiled a "Thanks," but inside I was thinking, "*That* doesn't sound like much fun!" By then I was part of a Wednesday evening knitting group, in which gabbing was what we all did while knitting, and I loved the socializing dimension of the get-together.

But as with most of my instinctive negative responses throughout my life, I soon had the humbling experience of discovering wisdom and truth in what I'd initially dismissed. That very evening, knitting in bed for the hour or so before sleeping—as had become my custom—I noticed my spirit engaged in a new way. Recalling Amanda's words about "knitting while praying," I found that each stitch invoked a prayer as it slipped through my fingers from the left needle to the right. It was a wordless prayer—just an awareness of Divine Presence. Creating each new stitch was like praying with prayer beads: the tactile passage of material through my fingers, my awakening mind and soul to the touch of transcendent reality.

Desert Fathers' Basket Weaving

A few weeks after my conversation with Amanda, my husband and I were paying a visit to a longtime friend who is a monk in the Trappist Abbey of the Genesee in western New York. The Trappists are an order of monks tracing their origin back to the sixth-century Benedict of Nursia, who is considered the founder of Christian monasticism. Trappists are contemplatives, which means that they dedicate their lives to prayerful contemplation of God. Their daily rhythm is marked by periods of communal and private contemplation.

As usual with our comfy visits over the years, George (my husband), Brother Anthony, and I were sitting under a tree in the fields outside the monastery chapel, catching up on each others' lives. At one point, George offered, "Well, Peggy has taken up knitting. That's something new."

I brushed it off. "Oh, that's girl stuff—you guys wouldn't be interested. But I do find it contemplative," I added, trying to make knitting sound meaningful to Brother Anthony's vocation.

"Absolutely," Brother Anthony immediately jumped in, to my surprise. "You know the Desert Fathers would weave baskets while they were at prayer."

I knew that the Desert Fathers were the fourth-century Christian hermits who chose a solitary life of prayer in the Egyptian desert, in order to devote themselves totally to union with God. But, no, I'd never heard about their basket weaving. What fun to find out. "Tell me more," I urged.

Brother Anthony elaborated. "Basket weaving helped their contemplative practice. The body is naturally restless, they said, so if you give it a focused activity, it settles down, calming the mind as well."

Now I was really gripped. "That's exactly what I've discovered in knitting!" How affirming to learn that I didn't "discover" it at all, but that these ancient masters of contemplative prayer had discovered it —had found that creating something with your hands could actually be an aid to settling the mind and spirit into deep repose.

The creative dimension was, in fact, what Brother Anthony then expanded on. "And for the Desert Fathers the creativity of weaving baskets added a contemplative dimension, too: the body busy with a peaceful creativity would be in harmony with the spirit creatively opening to the Divine Presence. In fact, since the *process* of basket weaving as prayer was what mattered to them, they sometimes burned the baskets after completing them."

Pick up your needles and
yarn for whatever project
calls to you at the moment—
nothing with a complicated
pattern, perhaps simply
a stockinette stitch piece
or garter stitch square. Sit
for fifteen minutes quietly
engaging in your knitting
activity. Focus all your
attention on what your
hands are creating.

The purpose of this exercise
is to give yourself the
opportunity to notice how
your mind and spirit can
become calm as your hands
do their creative work.

Musing now on Brother Anthony's account of the Desert Fathers keeping their hands busy with the creativity of basket weaving in order to settle their spirits into a creative opening to Divine Presence, I have to acknowledge that never has my inner being settled so quietly as it sometimes does now while knitting. My daily morning practice of sitting in what I've optimistically called "contemplative prayer" for over twenty-five years has never, I must confess, brought me to this inner peace of heightened awareness of Divine Presence. Mostly what it has brought me to is a heightened awareness of my to-do lists for the day or a heightened fussing over some interpersonal wrinkle that needed smoothing.

This failure of my contemplative practice is not the fault of my mentors. In fact, my spirituality has been formed by the Trappists themselves in the Benedictine tradition—by Brother Anthony and by my spiritual director of more than twenty-five years, Father William Shannon, himself a scholar of the Trappist monk Thomas Merton. Father Shannon has written several books drawing on Merton's contemplative wisdom, and I've chewed over and over the nuggets from his writing and those of Merton as well. But not until knitting have I experienced anything close to what Father Shannon calls, in his book *Silence on Fire*, the "prayer of awareness."

What Is Prayer?

Prayer. What *is* it, exactly? A book entitled *Knit One, Purl a Prayer* ought to define its key title term, I'd say.

But this is probably one of the hardest words in the language to pin down. In the most general way, any definition of prayer will have something to do with the relationship between human beings and the Divine—and with this relationship from the human point of view. Prayer, that is, is something that people do, not God. But beyond this general statement, definitions falter. Can we say that prayer is human speech to God? No, because much prayer is wordless. Prayer, I suggest, is our human longing for communication with the Divine.

In all major religious traditions this longing pours forth primarily as praise of the Divine. The Rig Veda, one of the ancient scriptures from which Hinduism was born, begins "I magnify God, the Divine Fire." Similarly, Mary the mother of Jesus, while pregnant and visiting her cousin Elizabeth in Luke's Gospel, begins her famous hymn praising God with "My soul magnifies the Lord" (Lk. 1:46). "Magnifies" here is sometimes translated as "glorifies." The point is the same no matter which word expresses it: awareness of God's graciousness moves people to grateful praise. So there is the Jewish prayer of praise on lighting the Sabbath candles at home: "Blessed are You, Lord our God, King of the universe, Who has made us holy through His commandments and commanded us to kindle the Sabbath light." And the core prayer of Christianity, the Lord's Prayer, starts with praise, or "hallowing" of God's name (that is, of God's very essence): "Our Father who art in heaven, hallowed be thy name." The comparable prayer for Muslims, recited at each of

their five daily prayer sessions, is the opening verse of the Qur'an, known as Surah al-Fatihah or The Opening, which begins "In the name of Allah, Most Gracious, Most Merciful. Praise be to Allah, the Cherisher and Sustainer of the Worlds; Most Gracious, Most Merciful; Master of the Day of Judgment."

But like the Lord's Prayer, which shifts halfway through from praise into petitioning God ("Give us this day our daily bread"), the Fatihah moves, toward its close, into petition: "You do we worship, and Your aid we seek. Show us the straight way." And petition is surely the form of prayer that we practice most often—no matter what our religion or even if we profess no religion. It is the cry of "Help!" to our transcendent Power. At the Fatihah's end, the longing for help is a prayer for divine guidance on the path of life. In Jewish worship, a privileged prayer is the Y'varech'cha, the high priestly prayer from the book of Numbers: "The Lord bless you and keep you; The Lord make his face to shine upon you, and be gracious to you; The Lord lift up his countenance upon you and give you peace" (6:24–26). A petition for peace and for divine light also informs the beloved Om prayer of Hindus: "Lead us from the unreal to the real, from darkness to light, from death to the Immortal One, Om peace peace peace." Many yoga traditions today open their practice with this prayer.

But prayer as petition can get out of hand. It's one thing to pray (as the Lord's Prayer ends) "Deliver us from evil"; it's another to pray for delivery of an email acceptance of my latest book proposal. In

Mark Twain's classic novel *The Adventures of Huckleberry Finn*, Huck starts off assuming that prayer is of the latter sort: simply asking for stuff you want to get. "But somehow I couldn't make it work," he complains. He'd prayed for a fish-line and hooks, but got only the line, and "It warn't any good to me without hooks." So in disgust he gives up on prayer. As well he should, since prayer is not bombarding God with our current wish lists.

All major spiritual traditions offer a model of prayer as, rather, *listening*. Perhaps most engagingly in the Bible is the episode (1 Kgs. 19:11–12) of the prophet Elijah hearing God's voice on Mount Horeb, the place where Moses had received the Ten Commandments. Fleeing from his enemies to a cave in the mountain, Elijah hears God announce that he will soon be passing by.

> Now there was a great wind, so strong that it was splitting mountains and breaking rocks in pieces before the Lord, but the Lord was not in the wind; and after the wind an earthquake, but the Lord was not in the earthquake; and after the earthquake a fire, but the Lord was not in the fire; and after the fire a sound of sheer silence.

It is in this "sound of sheer silence" (other translations say "a tiny whispering sound" or "a gentle whisper") that Elijah finally encounters God.

Knitting a Prayer

Anthony Bloom, an archbishop in the Eastern Orthodox Christian Church, recounts in his book *Beginning to Pray* his experience with a Russian woman in her nineties whom he visited in a nursing home. She begged his advice on how to pray, because her prayer life, she felt, had been fruitless. "These fourteen years I have been praying the Jesus Prayer almost continually, and never have I perceived God's presence at all." (The Jesus Prayer, central to Orthodox spirituality, is simply the line "Lord Jesus Christ, Son of God, have mercy upon me.") Bloom blurted out in response: "If you speak all the time, you don't give God a chance to place a word in." Then he suggested:

> Go to your room after breakfast, put it right, place your armchair in a strategic position that will leave behind your back all the dark corners . . . into which things are pushed so as not to be seen. Light your little lamp before the icon . . . [Orthodox homes traditionally have an icon altar, often with an image of the face of Christ.] Then take your knitting and for fifteen minutes knit before the face of God, but I forbid you to say one word of prayer. You just knit and try to enjoy the peace of your room.

At first, Bloom writes, the woman was suspicious that this advice was superficial. But when she returned to see him some time later, she announced, "It works!" Bloom was eager to hear her elaboration, so she told him how she had followed his instructions to neaten her room and then settle herself peacefully before her icon. She continued:

> After a while I remembered that I must knit before the face of God, and so I began to knit. And I became more and more aware of the silence. The needles hit the armrest of my chair, . . . there was nothing to bother about, . . . and then I perceived that this silence was not simply an absence of noise, but that the silence had substance. It was not absence of something but presence of something. . . . The silence around began to come and meet the silence in me. . . . At the heart of the silence there was He who is all stillness, all peace, all poise.

The woman had knit herself into the silent peace at the heart of the Divine Presence.

"The silence around began to come and meet the silence in me." The Desert Fathers explain that once our hearts can be silent enough to meet God's silence and peace, then our prayer can issue in thoughts or words or song or wordless gratitude. The vehicle of the communication with God doesn't matter; what matters is our openness of heart. One of the Desert *Mothers*, in fact—Mother Theodora—said, "It is good to live in peace, for the wise person practices perpetual prayer." And what is perpetual prayer? It is standing (or sitting) "with the mind in the heart before God." So said the great Russian Orthodox spiritual guide Bishop Theophan the Recluse, who drew his teaching from the Desert tradition. "Every prayer must come from the heart, and any other prayer is no prayer at all. Prayer-book prayers, your own prayers, and very short prayers, all must issue forth from the heart to God, seen before you."

This prayer of the heart, this opening of my spirit to whatever the Divine might be wishing to communicate to me: this is the form of prayer that knitting offers me.

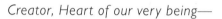

Creator, Heart of our very being—
May my heart open to your life beating within me,
May the ears of my heart hear your silently powerful presence,
May I live each moment in your peace.

Prayer Shawl Ministry

After settling for some weeks into this prayerful dimension of knitting that I'd discovered—and then had discovered that I hadn't at all "discovered" it, but had found for myself what has been known by the wisdom of ancient spiritual traditions—I remembered Amanda's comment about knitting prayer shawls: "You sit silently in a group," Amanda had explained, "and everyone knits while praying." By now I was humbly embarrassed by my initial dismissal of the value of knitting in prayerful silence. And I was curious about this thing called Prayer Shawl ministry. So I put "prayer shawl" into my computer's search engine—and sat dumbfounded watching page after page of entries pop up, nearly all linking to a Prayer Shawl group at a particular church congregation or parish around the country. I stopped after opening about fifty pages (and I was nowhere near the end of the listings), stopped in awe at what a powerfully healing movement the Prayer Shawl ministry has become.

It began as the brainchild—heartchild, really—of two women in Hartford, Connecticut, Janet Bristow and Victoria Galo. In 1997, after graduating together from a program in women's spirituality at the Hartford Seminary, Bristow and Galo pondered how to put into practice the newly deepened and broadened sense of God that they had experienced in their program. God, they had learned, has feminine dimensions: mothering, comforting, creatively caring. How could they carry this nurturing God out in the world to others?

Gradually, it came to them that their mutual love of knitting could be the vehicle for carrying forth God's loving care. And shawls seemed a natural. "Shawls," as Janet writes on their website, have been "made for centuries universal and embracing, symbolic of an inclusive, unconditionally loving, God. They wrap, enfold, comfort, cover, give solace, mother, hug, shelter and beautify." Vicky began by knitting a shawl in a spirit of prayerfulness for a friend going through a divorce, and then she brought the completed shawl to their women's group, where everyone spontaneously blessed it. And here the essence of Prayer Shawl ministry began.

Some fifteen years later, Janet and Vicky get a thousand hits a day on their website, shawlministry.com. The site is meant to encourage people everywhere to form their own Prayer Shawl groups, and that is exactly what has happened—as my Internet search for "prayer shawls" attests. Groups find their own ways to knit prayerfully. Sometimes it is in silence, as my friend Amanda said; sometimes it is with a sharing of details about the intended recipient of the shawl—a cousin with cancer, a neighbor recently widowed, a friend laid off from her job. And not all of the recipients being prayed for through knitting are suffering. Shawls are also made for celebration: of childbirth, of marriage, of retirement.

Generally, though, a Prayer Shawl group begins with a vocalized prayer. Many of these are collected on Janet and Vicky's website. This popular one by Cathleen O'Meara Murtha, DW, captures the spirit of them all:

As we gather in community to share our prayer, our stories,

the work of our hearts and hands, we pray for God's blessing on

our endeavors:

A blessing to my mind—

to be free to enter this time of contemplative activity . . .

A blessing to my hands—

to be the source of creating something of beauty and love . . .

A blessing to my soul—

to be open to the promptings of loving and caring . . .

A blessing to my yarn—

to be shaped into patterns of loving and caring . . .

A blessing to my needles—

    to be the holders of stitches as they become a whole garment . . .

A blessing to my knitting—

    to be a work of heart and hands, body and spirit . . .

A blessing on the one who will receive the fruit of my prayer and my

    knitting . . .

May this shawl be welcomed in the spirit in which it was knitted . . .

May we become one with the One who knitted each of us

    in our mother's womb . . .

I join my blessing, my prayer, and my knitting with women all over

    the earth in this common effort to bring healing and wholeness,

    comfort and celebration.

Inspired by first hearing about prayer shawls from Amanda, then finding for myself that the passing of yarn through my fingers over needles was like praying with beads, I've now come to sense something more happening—more than praying with beads—as I let my knitting become prayer. Like the Desert Fathers weaving their baskets to facilitate their contemplative prayer, like the knitters in Prayer Shawl ministries, I watch with astonished gratitude as a beautiful and useful object is created through this work of my hands.

PATTERNING YOUR PRAYER
Bookmark

A nice first pattern is a reversible bookmark;

I've designed a couple here.

Gauge: 5 or 6 stitches = 1"

Yarn: Choose a DK weight yarn, which is thin enough to fit smoothly in your book. Berroco Comfort DK is a nice choice because of its sheen.

Needles: Use needles size US6 or the size needed to obtain gauge.

For beginners: Your local yarn store will show you how to cast on, how to do the basic knit stitch, and how to bind off when you're done. You can also find many excellent instructional videos by searching the Internet.

Pattern for beginners:

Cast on 10 stitches.

Knit every row (called garter stitch) until you have the length of bookmark you want. Mine is 7" inches long.

Bind off, leaving at least a 6" tail.

To make a tassel for your bookmark:

Take a yarn needle and thread the tail onto it.

Weave the needle along the bound-off stitches until you get to the center of your bookmark.

Cut two 8" pieces of your yarn.

Fold them in half and tie them around your tail at its base.

Cut all 5 strands to the same length.

Pattern for experienced knitters:

Cast on 10 stitches, then try the minirib pattern below. This will keep you interested while still being repetitive enough to be meditative.

Rows 1 and 2: Knit.

Row 3: P2, *K2, P2; repeat from *.

Row 4: K2, *P2, K2; repeat from *.

Rows 5 and 6: Knit.

Row 7: Repeat Row 4.

Row 8: Repeat Row 3.

Six repeats of rows 1–8 will give you a good length for a bookmark. Make tassel according to the instructions.

TWO

Knit One, Purl a Passage

If I knew the pattern . . .

I would knit the dictionary into your socks

—Willa Cline, "I Would Knit You Socks"

The Prayer Is in the Pause

I was raised in a loving, agnostic household. I remember as a teenager feeling an emptiness on Sundays, a restlessness, the sense of wanting to be somewhere but not knowing where, not guessing what might fill my emptiness. As a young adult, I became aware that the restlessness was a longing for religious faith . . . and thus I began a long conversion process that culminated in my baptism in the Roman Catholic Church in 1983, when I was thirty-nine years old. My husband, George, whose childhood home had been similarly devoid of religious practice, joined me throughout the conversion process and in baptism.

During the months of preparation leading up to our baptism, a friend took us one Sunday afternoon to the Trappist Abbey of the Genesee, which I mentioned in chapter 1. George and I had never visited a monastery; nor did we know anything about monastic tradition or practice. I can still recall my wonderment as we sat in the chapel while the monks slowly chanted the psalms of Evening

Prayer in the dimming twilight. Trappist monks chant a selection of the psalms seven times each day. And at each of these prayer times, they pause between the psalms. It was in these pauses that I sensed a reverberation wholly new to me: something alive that I can only call the movement of the Spirit. When we left the chapel, George commented that he had never before experienced a silence of such fullness, such substance.

Because of this experience, we decided to make a retreat at the Abbey during Lent before our upcoming Easter baptism. That's when we first met Brother Anthony, who was retreat-master at the time. From him we learned the beginnings of how to pray the psalms as the monks do, letting the silence after each psalm become a rich pause of connection with a particular image or phrase, or with the psalm's overall message about God's loving care for all creatures. George and I began praying together at home three times a day—morning, evening, and bedtime—modeling our prayer on the monks'.

Without even trying to, I found that I was gradually memorizing certain psalm lines. Favorite lines, those that spoke most meaningfully to me, would settle into my mind and heart and make a home there, always ready to bubble up when needed. "Be still and know that I am God" from Psalm 46; "As a deer longs for flowing streams, so my soul longs for you, O God" from Psalm 42; "Have mercy on me, O God, according to your steadfast love" from Psalm 51.

Meanwhile, we had begun spending one Sunday a month at the Abbey, to soak in the communal prayer and to visit with Brother

Anthony, who informally took on the role of our spiritual director. Once when we were talking about learning the psalms "by heart," Brother Anthony said, "Oh, well, then you'd enjoy Cassian." Cassian? "He was one of the earliest monks—fourth to early fifth century—and he developed the practice of praying with Scripture 'by heart,' which was carried on by Benedict, the founder of our monastic life."

So I bought an edition of Cassian's writings right then, at the Abbey bookstore. And yes, there it was: Cassian's insistence that when we chant the psalms with discerning attention and let them reverberate through our being in the subsequent pause, the words enter our "veins and marrow"—so that we come to know the psalms not as mere words but with the same "feeling of heart" that generated them. "As our feelings become our teachers, we touch the words not as things which are heard, but rather as things perceived; we give birth to them in feeling from within our own heart."

This renewed birth within us of the sacred lines happens in the *pause* after reading or singing a psalm. For Cassian, the prayer is in the pause. No wonder George had heard, on our first visit to the Abbey, a rich substance in the silence after the monks' chanting of each psalm. The silent pause was where the action was: the action of conforming our own hearts to the divine word.

Knitting Along the Lines

Over the years after my baptism, as I began to broaden my spiritual studies to enfold sacred texts of other faiths—the Hindu classic Bhagavad-Gita, Buddhist Sutras, the Tao Te Ching of ancient Chinese wisdom, Islam's Qur'an—I'd find lines in them all that I wanted to know by heart. To know, that is, in Cassian's way of knowing: pausing with them in the meditative way that would draw them into the core of my being.

So it was only natural that, after I'd discovered how knitting could be a meditative activity, a special line from my heart's storehouse would surface to my mind as a mantra while I'd knit along a row.

In chapter 1, I wrote of prayer as *listening* to what the Divine is trying to say to us. There I stressed the inner silence that we need in order to hear the divine word. But the divine message—or eternal wisdom—also communicates through sacred texts. Issuing from our inner silence, words from these texts can bubble up if they have become integral to our being.

Some of my own favorite lines, which have become silent mantras as I knit, are these:

From the Beatitudes, this promise of a cosmic exchange of blessings: "Blessed are the merciful, for they will receive mercy" (Matt. 5:7).

From the Qur'an, this tender blending of imperative and blessing: "Do good, as Allah has been good to you" (Surah 28:77).

From Shambhala Buddhism's "Dedication of Merit," this prayer, which also implicitly draws us toward the goodness within our souls: "May all become compassionate and wise."

And from the Hebrew prophet Isaiah, relating God's message to a beloved people: "Give ear and come to me; listen, that you may live" (Isa. 55:3, NIV).

It's not only the message of all these lines that moves me to internalize them, to learn them by heart. It's also their rhythms in these particular translations (for all, of course, were originally composed in languages other than English). Knitting is a rhythmic activity, and its rhythms naturally bring to mind words that flow along the body's beat.

Lines like those quoted, ones that I already know by heart, can become—as I've said—a mantra while I knit. But if I want to learn by heart a new line, I remember Cassian's insight that the prayer is in the pause. So, with my knitting in hand, I read the line from a book; then I let the meditative rhythm of knitting become the internal pause in which the new words can reverberate and eventually settle into the core of my being. I knit the words of wisdom into my heart.

Scriptural Knits and Other Crafts

"You knit me together in my mother's womb."

This line from Psalm 139 is quoted on just about every knitting website that talks about the prayerful dimension of knitting. The whole verse (Ps. 139:13–14) addresses God in praise of the glorious divine creativity:

For it was you who formed my inward parts;
you knit me together in my mother's womb.
I praise you, for I am fearfully and wonderfully made.
Wonderful are your works; that I know very well.

Meditation

Take up your knitting, work that is comfortable for you to do without much attention—even work that you consider boring! Choose a single line or phrase from whatever sacred text or Scripture is meaningful to you. Read the line or phrase aloud, slowly. Then hold these words in your heart as you knit along one row, saying the words silently as a mantra. The purpose of this exercise is to give you the opportunity to knit a line of wisdom into your heart.

In *The Christian Century*, Patrick J. Willson offers a marvelous reading of these lines.

> Though we may evade knowing God by carelessness
> or indifference, we cannot escape God knowing us. It
> is in our DNA spun into that swirling double helix that
> determines us and apparently predestines us in ways we
> shudder to imagine. God's knowing is woven into the
> textile of our living because God is a weaver and a knitter
> too. In ancient Israel, as in most cultures, weaving and
> knitting were done by women; the psalmist pictures the
> Lord doing her knitting in a mother's womb.

For Christians, who are offered union with God and one another in Christ, the New Testament occasionally images this union as a "knitting together" in love. In Paul's Letter to the Ephesians (4:15–16), the Greek word describing people's joining with one another in Christ can be translated as "bind together" or "knit together":

> Speaking the truth in love, we must grow up in every way
> into him who is the head, into Christ, from whom the
> whole body, *joined and knit together* by every ligament with
> which it is equipped, as each part is working properly, pro-
> motes the body's growth in building itself up in love.

In the Sanskrit of the Bhagavad-Gita, the multidimensional word *yoga* (literally "yoking together") carries similar meanings and more. *Yoga,* as we're familiar with the term today, refers to a set of physical meditation techniques aimed at integration of the self. In the Bhagavad-Gita, any such integration finds its fulfillment in the self's "yoking" with the Divine.

When the mind is resting in the stillness of the prayer of

Yoga, and by the grace of the Spirit sees the Spirit and

   therein finds fulfillment;

Then the seeker knows the joy of Eternity . . .

Thus joy supreme comes to the Yogi whose heart is still,

   whose passions are peace, who is pure from sin, who

   is one with Brahman, with God.

So the Divine has been seen as supreme creator, craftsperson, artist: sometimes as weaver or spinner or knitter—and sometimes as potter. In the creation stories of indigenous peoples worldwide, the Divine is often imaged as creating the world from clay. And a beloved biblical passage is the prophet Jeremiah's likening of God to a potter, with humankind as the clay in the potter's hands. At God's command to "go down to the potter's house," Jeremiah recounts that:

I went down to the potter's house, and there he was

working at his wheel. The vessel he was making of clay

was spoiled in the potter's hand, and he reworked it into

another vessel, as seemed good to him. Then the word of

the Lord came to me: ". . . Just like the clay in the potter's

hand, so are you in my hand, O house of Israel." (Jer. 18:1–6)

Canadian poet Sarah Klassen has written a poem, "The Potter," that reenvisions Jeremiah's scene of visiting the potter's house. Klassen's divine potter, who is female, shapes her clay into a lovely bowl but then suddenly squashes it without a word, implying that it didn't meet her mind's vision. The puzzled visitors, however, are then unexpectedly treated by the potter to tea and cookies. The whole poem is an engaging reflection on creativity's unpredictability and also its graciousness.

Prayer

Creator, Divine Artist,
Maker of us all—
Mold us to your liking,
Help us to live the beauty
Worthy of your Art.

Knitting Poems

Tucson writer Deborah B., who blends poetry and prose in her work in experimental ways, sent me an email about how poetry and knitting interact for her. A young mom, Deborah slips in her creative work while her toddler naps. "Peggy," she began, "here are the thoughts I managed to write during naptime, as I was knitting my featherweight cardigan—I go back and forth between knitting and writing, though I guess they are really the same thing for me somehow, which I try to describe here":

Knitting is a transportive act, a vehicle for creative thought. No matter how quickly I knit, my mind travels at a speed rivaling that of light. Sometimes, when my daughter naps, I bring out a cup of tea and book of poetry. Eleni Sikelianos's *Body Clock* has been a recent favorite. I read a few lines, just until an image or the sound of a phrase snags me. I sip my tea and set off down the next row of my knitting. Needles transform a strand of yarn into fabric, fabric into weight on my lap. My mind tumbles words I've read and I knit quicker to the rhythm. The snag turns into a tear that I fall through (like Alice tumbling down the rabbit hole). On the other side of the tear, I hang—haphazard and marvelous!—from my knitting, in a place filled with light, texture, the edges of sounds. I dip into a million words from this place and pull myself out to the other side for another sip of tea. Meanwhile, words glide across the needles. I open my laptop and put down a fast poem. Then back to the yarn. My mind craves it as much as my fingers do; silky merino in my hands results in words knit together. Knitting ferries me into a wonderland of saturated colors, and blissful textures. Rapture rushes, and I am transported. When I say, "Just one more row," I mean I need more of this peculiar act that is other acts all working together to set me at perfect ease and edgy mind-winding. I have not yet been knitting a full year—so much lost time to make up for.

"Words glide across the needles." I'm not a poet, as Deborah is. But I'm an avid reader of poetry. And, like Deborah, I've discovered that the combination of knitting while reading poetry can be transportive. Where I'm carried off to is not so much into Deborah's wondrously exuberant creativity as into a meditative state.

As I take out my knitting, I open whatever book of poetry I'm currently reading. Then I experience something similar to what I described earlier, where I talked about knitting into my heart some lines from sacred texts. So I'll read a line from the poem, then hold the line in my mind as I knit along the row to its rhythm. When the words have settled deep inside me, I pause in my knitting to look at the poem's next line, then return to knit with it in the same way.

This is how I've mused on Sarah Klassen's "The Potter." And also on Scott Cairns's pensive "Evening Prayer," from his collection *Compass of Affection*. With startling candidness, Cairns's poem draws us into the evening of human suffering and doubt ("And what *would* you pray in the troubled midst / of this our circular confusion save / that the cup be taken away?"); and since evening is when I usually knit, the poem's probing questions resonate with special relevance. "What *would* you pray at the approach of this / late evening? What ask? And of whom?"

"What ask? And of whom?" The questions click along the row as my needles make each stitch.

Or I'll knit with any of the poem-meditations in Mary Lou Kownacki's *Between Two Souls*, where she pairs a poem by the nineteenth-century Zen monk Ryokan with a reflection from her contemporary monastic life. "My daily fare: playing with the village children," he writes. She responds: "My weekly fare: teaching poetry to children." He goes on: "This cloth ball in my sleeve is more valuable than a thousand pieces of gold." She counters: "A bold phrase or image / Pops out of a child's hand and struts across the page." To enact their paired voices as I knit, I read Ryokan for the right-side row of stitches, then turn my needles to the wrong-side row for Kownacki's responding lines.

It's true that I can read a poem as a slow-paced meditation without the help of knitting. Over the years of practicing a meditative reading of poetry, however, I've never fully succeeded in keeping myself from rushing on to a poem's next line. But because knitting is a repetitive motion like a mantra, it naturally lures the mind into a meditative state. And poetry's lines then slip comfortably into the mind's mantric motion.

Except when I drop a stitch by mistake, of course, or have to figure out a complicated new pattern. Then prosaic reality takes over with a vengeance.

Poets Knitting

"I've often thought of knitting as being like writing poetry—making something out of tight little lines with no extra slack so that the lines work together to make a complex pattern. A long blank verse poem even looks like a scarf—which would, by extension, mean a sonnet is kind of like a fancy potholder."

Hannah Faith Notess wrote this delightful, insightful comment in response to one of my posts about poetry and knitting at *Good Letters*, the blog of *Image* journal. Hannah is an editor of Seattle Pacific University's *Response* magazine and a poet herself. Other contemporary poets, too, have made connections between knitting and their poetic craft. Some write poems specifically about knitting. Others use knitting as the source of metaphor for their musings on life.

Probably the most famous poem about knitting is "Ode to My Socks," by the Chilean poet Pablo Neruda. Spinning image after image of a pair of wool socks knit for him ("soft as rabbits," "two long sharks," "two cannons," and more), then for his unworthiness to wear them ("my feet seemed to me unacceptable / like two decrepit firemen"), Neruda ends by celebrating the socks' magnificence. Since the socks are a pair, they double beauty—"and what is good is doubly good."

Playing off of Neruda's "Ode," Willa Cline of Kansas composed "I Would Knit You Socks," posted on her website in 2005.

If I knew the pattern . . .
I would knit the dictionary into your socks,
the lives of the saints, and
the meanings of dreams.

And I would wind them 'round with sunlight and honey, . . .
Not knowing how to knit such socks,
I write poetry.
and practice.

If Neruda's is the most famous poem about knitting, literature's most famous knitter—Madame Defarge—inspires other poems. Defarge (or LeFarge, as she is sometimes named) is the sinister revolutionary who in Charles Dickens's *A Tale of Two Cities* sits by the guillotine knitting in code the names of the aristocracy who will be next to lose their heads. My favorite of the Defarge poems is one posted on a blog by Joelle, who doesn't give her last name but calls herself "A soul longing . . . to live in Love, to be more and more alive to God's presence, to simply be." She titles the poem "Knitting":

. . . Madame Guillotine

effortlessly decapitates

a second of the past for every

stitch.

A moment of impatience, knit one.

A heartbeat of resentment, knit another.

Fear, knit again and cross the strand.

A good poem will always surprise, and here the surprise is the poet's identification with the deadly knitter:

Madame LeFarge,

moi,

sits: still, but for the

metallic clink and flash of needles . . .

Startlingly effective, too, are the poem's refrain-variations, which punctuate with quiet longing the violence around them:

Knit three,

purl three,

epitome

of simplicity. . . .

Knit three,

purl three,

Trinity,

flow in me.

This is a poem about knitting, yes, but also about more: about fears, longings, prayer. Other poems that on the surface are about knitting also probe life's depths. I think of Sally Bittner Bonn's "Catapult, Cull, Collide & Commune," dedicated to "the women I knit with":

we stitch and bleed

knit and knead

our fists into our chests . . .

we shape shoulders

we work threads into fabric

we bleed with the moon . . .

though some sweaters can be knit in six days

there is more than one truth

binding us to the Earth

bind off, weave in the ends, block the garment

we stitch and bleed

knit and knead

our fists into our chests

we press two fingers to our sternums and lift

to keep this structure from caving in

Bonn's poem, with its powerfully crafted edginess, uses knitting to reflect on what it means to be a woman living in connection to others and to the earth.

Finally, there are poems where knitting comes in solely as metaphor. In Jeanne Murray Walker's "Sister Storm," knitting—as for Bonn—becomes an image for human and cosmic connectedness. Walker's title recalls St. Francis's "Canticle of Brother Sun," where Francis praises God through "Sister Moon," "Brother Fire," "Sister Water," and so on. Walker's "Sister Storm," however, is violent and destructive—definitely not, in the poet's view, an element through which to praise God. The poet talks bravely back to the lightning storm that is raging:

I defy you. Leave us alone

and tell your ugly cousin, war,

to leave our kids alone.

I write for all of us.

With life I write this.

I write with death.

And then comes the surprisingly constructive image with which

the poet defies the storm:

My house is knit to other houses,

living rooms hooked to front yards,

neighborhood to neighborhood,

hooked to that bright creative engine,

to whose rule, before the sun, moon

and stars, we hold out our hands.

Knitting is formed by a series of loops "hooked" to subsequent

loops. Walker takes this core image and expands it dramatically. First

it's the image for her treasured connectedness to the people around

her; then further out the image connects "neighborhood to neighbor-

hood"; then in the poem's closing lines above, the poet projects the

image out to cosmic size. Her life and those of her neighbors and the

neighborhood's neighbors—that is, of all people in their connected-

ness—are knit to the creative force of "sun, moon / and stars." I hear an echo here of the final line of Dante's *Divine Comedy*: to that "love that moves the sun and the other stars." This cosmic, divine love, in Walker's vision, knits us all together in a creative work that overpowers the forces of destructiveness and death.

Meditation

Choose any line or phrase from the poems quoted in this chapter and reflect on how it expresses something about what knitting can mean for you.

The purpose of this exercise is to enjoy how poets can knit our lives into their words.

PATTERNING YOUR PRAYER
Happy Life Scarf
by Sviatlana Harnizonava

Sviatlana Harnizonava created this Happy Life Scarf inspired by slip-stitch patterns of her native Russia. Its deep-color framing of multicolor yarn gives a stunning stained-glass effect. For a brighter look, I played with her pattern to make a slimmer scarf with the solid black in the background. I used Noro Silk Garden with Noro black cashmere. You can create your own variations of this basic slip-stitch pattern, which takes just enough attention to keep you focused while allowing the rhythm of alternating 9 and 5 stitches to underlie any mantra you might be knitting with.

Gauge: 10 stitches = 2"

Yarn: worsted weight, 2 colors (one solid, one multistriping), 200 yds of each color.

Needles: US7 or size to obtain gauge.

M = multistriping yarn.

D = dark solid color yarn.

S = slip stitch purlwise with yarn always held to *wrong side* (WS).

With D: cast-on 37 sts.

With D:

Row 1 (RS): Knit across row.

Row 2 (WS): K9, P5, K9, P5, K9.

With M:

Row 3 (RS): K9, S1, P1, S1, P1, S1, K9, S1, P1, S1, P1, S1, K9.

Row 4 (WS): K9, S1, K1, S1, K1, S1, K9, S1, K1, S1, K1, S1, K9.

With D:

Row 5 (RS): Repeat Row 1.

Row 6 (WS): Repeat Row 2.

With M:

Row 7 (RS): Repeat Row 3.

Row 8 (WS): Repeat Row 4.

With D:

Row 9 (RS): Knit across row.

Row 10 (WS): K2, P5, K9, P5, K9, P5, K2.

With M:

Row 11 (RS): K2, S1, P1, S1, P1, S1, K9, S1, P1, S1, P1, S1, K9, S1, P1, S1, P1, S1, K2.

Row 12 (WS): K2, S1, K1, S1, K1, S1, K9, S1, K1, S1, K1, S1, K9, S1, K1, S1, K1, S1, K2.

With D:

Row 13 (RS): Repeat Row 9.

Row 14 (WS): Repeat Row 10.

With M:

Row 15 (RS): Repeat Row 11.

Row 16 (WS): Repeat Row 12.

Repeat Rows 1–16 until you reach the desired length. End with dark solid color rows 1 and 2. Bind off.

THREE

Knit One, Purl a Community

Knit, from Old English meaning "to knot." By Middle English, also figurative for "uniting intimately."
—*Oxford English Dictionary*

Close-Knit Relationships

Around the mid-nineteenth century, the most common social gathering in the British countryside was the neighborhood knitting group. Here's how it is described in an 1844 book, *The Rural Life of England:*

As soon as it becomes dark and the usual business of the day is over and the young children are put to bed, [residents] rake or put out the fire, take their cloaks and lanterns, and set out with their knitting to the house of the neighbour where the sitting falls in rotation, for it is a regularly circulating assembly from house to house through the particular neighbourhood. The whole troop of neighbours being collected, they sit and knit, sing knitting songs and tell knitting stories . . . till after twelve o'clock. All this time their knitting goes on with unremitting speed.

Today, small groups of knitters in much of the world have a "regularly circulating assembly from house to house." They don't meet *every* evening, as in rural England two centuries ago; more likely, it's every week or two. In the groups I've been part of, we don't "sing knitting songs" or knit (most of us) "with unremitting speed." But our gathering serves much the same purpose as these nineteenth-century groups: socializing while knitting nonstop. In fact, the knitting actually *enhances* the socializing, the bonding.

Often the venue for gathering to knit is not a home but the neighborhood yarn shop. Tucson's Kiwi Knitting Company, for instance, has Knit Night every Monday. When I've lived in Tucson for the winters, I've enjoyed Kiwi's Monday evening camaraderie. In the shop's spacious back room, ten to twenty regular customers gather to chat while they knit, turning to each other or to shop owner Lynn Davis for help when needed. The room is abuzz with several simultaneous conversations: sometimes about knitting, sometimes about what's going on in everyone's lives. "Hey, you're home from college—how's the first year going?" "Wow, what a spectacularly beautiful afghan that is turning out to be." "What's dress-up wear in Tucson? I know: [several people at once] You wear the jeans without the holes in them." "Well, I've spent the evening knitting four rows and ripping out the four rows, so at least I'm even."

Though knitting groups occasionally include men, in the United States and Canada today they are predominantly women's groups. Molly Oliver, practitioner of India's ancient system of self-healing called Ayurveda, talks about the sense of community created when women knit together:

> Something happens when *women* sit around and *make* things. *Doing* side by side *while* talking creates a special feeling, a bond. Ayurveda would explain it in terms of the autonomic nervous system: repetitive motion is soothing, recalling our being rocked in a cradle, or in the womb. This sense of safety lets your guard down. It *slows* us down from our crazy pace of life and its pressures. Knitting demands that we *stop*, sit down.

Out of this sense of safety created by knitting, friendships develop. Testimony to this phenomenon came from a professor of religious studies, Christine Bochen, as she was sitting between her longtime friend Sheila and her former student Meghan, both now members of her knitting group:

> Knitting creates friendships. Sheila and I have knit together for a long time. Then I met younger people [nodding toward Meghan] who moved the knitting-connection across generations. So knitting for me is all about sharing, relationship. We become "close-knit." Knitting is about community and friendship. It's both personal and communal.

The discussion in which Christine made this comment was held at Yarn Boutique, my neighborhood knit shop in my hometown of Rochester, New York. There could be no more appropriate venue for Christine's words on the communal dimension of knitting. Yarn Boutique's owner, Amelia Templar, had offered her shop for me to hold a discussion among knitters on what knitting means in their lives—part of my research for this book. A dozen or so of us were seated on the couch and comfy chairs surrounding a coffee table covered with knitting books and knitting supplies, the area usually occupied by customers who come by daily to "sit and knit," sometimes forming friendships right around that table. On the table was a bright-pink paper giving the hospital address of a customer (one of the "sit and knitters") who was seriously ill—so that others could send her cards.

Activity

Visit your local yarn shop to see if you are comfortable with the community there.

Local yarn stores like Yarn Boutique and Kiwi Knitting are literally creators of community. First, a local yarn store is locally owned. How many American businesses can make that claim? And when the owner is as welcoming as Amelia or Lynn, word gets around that this is a place where knitters can be nurtured in and through their knitting: nurtured in their craft (by staff members available to help solve a knotty problem, and by classes in knitting techniques and projects), and nurtured in their lives as well. A novel popular among knitters, Kate Jacobs's *The Friday Night Knitting Club*, is barely exaggerated in its gripping story of how a fictional yarn shop brings into life-and-death intimacy the most unlikely group of people.

At the close of the previous chapter, I quoted from Jeanne Murray Walker's "Sister Storm":

My house is knit to other houses,

living rooms hooked to front yards,

neighborhood to neighborhood . . .

Walker is of course using knitting as a metaphor—for human connectedness. But now in this chapter I've talked about how knitting *literally* bonds us, actually creates friendships and community. So I want to play with Walker's lines, recasting them this way:

My life is knit to other lives,

as we circulate through our living rooms,

or in the yarn shop where we knit together

to be knit together.

Giving Oneself Away

It's important to me that I not knit only for me. I knit to *connect* with other people. So when someone on the block has a baby, I knit a baby blanket as a gift—like a

grandmother would. And if I don't know a particular person who needs something, I'll give my knitted things away—like hats to the city schools for the kids there.

Becky White was sitting with me on her living room couch as she told me this. A recently retired widow, she was dressed in a red sweater twinset with pewter heart-shaped earrings and matching pin. She'd prepared for our interview by pulling together her thoughts on what knitting means in her life. As I listened to her gentle, heartfelt words, I began to see her jewelry as genuinely representing her inner being.

Becky had invited me to her home for this interview in response to an announcement I'd made at that month's Rochester Knitting Guild meeting. About two hundred knitters attend each meeting, coming from as far as a hundred miles away. I'd announced at the meeting that I was writing a book on the spirituality of knitting and that I welcomed speaking with anyone who was willing to share experiences or thoughts on the topic.

Another respondent was seventy-two-year-old Rollie Abkowitz. Rollie told me:

When I knit, I love to see the finished projects. And then giving them away. Giving to others is like giving to yourself. I just heard that a friend out of town has been diagnosed with cancer. I've had a chunky yarn small blanket that I made a while ago and use as a lap robe. I immediately put it in the mail to her. Giving away my knitting is a way to communicate with others—like a big, warm hug.

The Knitting Guild itself sponsors projects that send big, warm hugs out to the larger community, including three hundred pairs of mittens donated to an inner city public library at Christmas, helmet liners for soldiers overseas, and lap robes donated to hospitals for their patients.

Knitting guilds around the world do the same. As do an astounding array of other organizations, many of which are compiled in Betty Christiansen's book *Knitting for Peace: Make the World a Better Place One Stitch at a Time.* One of the volunteer outreach endeavors that Christiansen features, Project Linus (projectlinus.org), collects hand-knit blankets for traumatized and critically ill children across the country. "A Project Linus blanket is like a portable hug," says founder Karen Loucks. (There's that knitted hug again.) Lots of local yarn stores participate in outreach projects like this one. In fact, I first learned about Project Linus from a corner devoted to it at Tucson's Kiwi Knitting Company.

Nearly eighty more volunteer organizations that have invented creative projects for giving themselves away through knitting are linked to by the online knitting magazine *Interweave Knits.* For instance, there's Warm the World (warmtheworld.org), based in Cañon City, Colorado, which makes knitted and crocheted blankets for a wide range of people in need—from patients in a hospice close to home in

Colorado to families in faraway South Africa. There's Tiny Stitches (tinystitches.com), based in Gwinnett County, Georgia, which collects knitted and sewn clothing for babies born to families in financial need. There's Global Knit (globalknit.org), based in central Ohio, with the motto "warming the world one stitch at a time"; they distribute hand-knit and crocheted clothing to at-risk children all over the globe, making their first project for disabled youth in Bulgaria. There's Sharing Our Gifts (sharingourgifts.org), based evidently in cyberspace; a combination of blog and knitting/sewing project, it chooses a charity in a different state each month to make gifts for. State number three was the Oklahoma Brain Tumor Foundation; state number five was a Florida homeless shelter.

Following these links, I feel as if I'm being wafted through the astonishingly creative work of the Holy Spirit. None of the groups listed above claims a religious grounding. Yet undeniably, a spirit of creative giving motivates and sustains them all.

As a Christian, I see them all living out the prayer of the shawl ministry at First Presbyterian Church of Normal, Illinois: "Gracious God, we give thanks for the gift of our hands. Give us the grace to see our hands as you see them, as instruments of grace and life. May the knitting of our hands be the knitting of our hearts. Use our hands, O God, to carry out your works of mercy and love."

Knit something to give away. Notice whether, as you're knitting, your spirit is engaged differently than it is when you're knitting something for yourself.

Picking Up the Threads of the Past

Near the opening of Sir Philip Sidney's classic work *Arcadia*, first published in 1590, a shipwrecked young man is taken for refuge to Arcadia, which is described in lush, pastoral terms:

There were hills which garnished their proud heights with stately trees: . . . meadows, enameled with all sorts of eye-pleasing flowers: thickets, which being lined with most pleasant shade, were witnessed to by the cheerful deposition of many well-tuned birds: . . . here a shepherd boy piping, as though he should never be old: there a young shepherdess knitting, and withal singing, and it seemed that her voice comforted her hands to work, and her hands kept time to her voice's music.

So we know that knitting was a pastime in sixteenth-century England. And from Italian paintings of the Madonna from as early as the fourteenth century—such as the charming domestic scene of *The Holy Family* by Ambrogio Lorenzetti depicting Mary knitting while the young boy Jesus affectionately holds her arm and Joseph speaks to them both—we know that knitting was common enough then to be recognized as an image of domestic harmony.

This isn't the place to recount the history of knitting. Richard Rutt's *A History of Hand Knitting* does this delightfully, with the amateur's passion for his subject. (Rutt's career was as an Anglican bishop in England; he learned knitting at his grandfather's knee.) And for the changing role of knitting in American women's lives, the indispensable resource is Anne L. Macdonald's *No Idle Hands: The Social History of American Knitting*. Macdonald's book is a gold mine of quotations from and about women from colonial days into the 1980s. She demonstrates that, while the purpose of knitting has changed—from the necessity to clothe one's household, through the patriotic fervor to warm our soldiers in successive wars, to the fun and relaxation and camaraderie that have motivated knitters since the 1970s—American women have continually knit.

Many knitters today consciously carry on the craft of their forebears. Isabel Morrison, my friend and my first knitting mentor, told me: "One of the reasons I knit traditional patterns is because my parents grew up in Scotland. I return there and I bring home that yarn. I knit to connect myself with my ancestors."

Knitter Liza Steffen, whom I met at my Rochester yarn store, grew up in Russia. She recalled, "My grandmother would come to our house to knit socks with the other women. I loved to sit at their feet. My ears got big, listening to their stories."

When I visited Molly Oliver, the Ayurvedic practitioner I mentioned earlier, to interview her for this book, Molly showed me a chair-throw in her living room; it was an unusually shaped piece of knitting, much wider at one end than the other. "My mom had this project in her home," Molly recalled, "and anyone who came in could knit on it—to learn knitting or just for fun." Molly saved it because of its history. It is a unique, concrete witness to the communal dimension of knitting.

I don't have a personal connection to knitters of the past as Isabel and Liza and Molly do. None of my ancestors knit that I know of. But one of my most treasured spiritual forebears did knit: the medieval mystic Julian of Norwich. Over the decades, I've returned to Julian for her radical vision of God's infinite love for us, a love so all-embracing that we are one with God in our very essence. "One-ed" is actually a verb for Julian's Middle English, and she draws on her own daily knitting as an image for how this oneness with God can be. God wishes us to be aware, she writes,

> that mankind's dearworthy soul was preciously knit to Him in the creation—and this knot is subtle and so powerful that it is one-ed into God. In this one-ing it is made endlessly holy. Furthermore, He wishes us to be aware that all the souls that shall be saved in heaven without end are knit and one-ed in this one-ing, and made holy in this holiness.

When I knit now with Julian's words in mind, I sense that I'm picking up and continuing the ongoing knitting of women for centuries past, as all of us are knit together by God into the divine life that stretches from before time and into eternity.

A Yarn to Share

During that discussion at Yarn Boutique about what knitting means in our lives, the conversational energy had revved up, with everyone stimulated by others' quick-coming comments on how knitting could be at once meditative, creative, solitary, communal—and then Christine threw in, "It's like we all have a yarn to share." As we all howled with laughter at the pun, Sue Sayre added wryly: "Yarns are stories knitters tell each other around the fire."

The yarns we share: Becky White had said to me in her home, talking about her experience with knitting, "I've never done anything else where there's so much give and take—so much sharing."

Lots of this sharing is done in person, in the home-based knitting groups, the yarn stores, and the knitting guilds that I've talked about. But lots, too, is done these days online. In 2000, when the Internet was young, knitter Clara Parkes began her *Knitter's Review* weekly newsletter, offering information on supplies, knitting books, and yarns at knittersreview. com. By 2010, she had 35,000 subscribers and an interactive forum where knitters could talk together in cyberspace. Meanwhile, a truly countless number of individual blogs by knitters has emerged. One site alone, bloggers.com, hosts 988,000 bloggers who identify knitting as a prime topic for their posts. Another popular blogsite, wordpress.com, pulls up 278,057 posts when I search the word *knitting*.

A favorite blog for knitters is the Yarn Harlot (yarnharlot.ca/blog/), by Canadian master-knitter and writer Stephanie Pearl-McPhee. A marvel of creativity and wit, Stephanie uses her blog mainly to journal about her current knitting projects, complete with photos putting the knitted work in artistic settings. She is so comfortably humorous about her work and her life that readers feel they are her close friends sitting around the kitchen table with her. A post simply on her springtime love of knitting with green (June 10, 2010), illustrated by a string of differently angled photos of a leafy-patterned green scarf she'd just knit, stimulated over a hundred comments. Typically Stephanie gets so many comments, with some respondents conversing with each other, that she has actually created a community of knitters at her blog.

But the site deliberately set up for knitters to share their yarns (in both senses of the word) is the astoundingly successful Ravelry.com, known to knitters everywhere just as "Ravelry." Ravelry requires only a username and password to join, and once a member, you are in contact with more than a million knitters around the world. Whenever I log on, between two and three thousand members are on the site at that moment, from countries on five different continents.

And why do I log on? It might be to find a lacy scarf pattern (search "lace scarf" and 114 patterns come up, many of them free downloads). It might be to see what other knitters think about a sweater pattern I want to use for my granddaughters (search the pattern name, and every Raveler who has done this pattern pops up, many with useful notes on how they altered the pattern or found errors in it). It might be because I'm stuck on something and need technical help (how to do a certain increase, how to fix a mistake, how to do a provisional cast-on: whatever the question, other Ravelers instantly reply with helpful tips). It might be because I want to chat with knitters about a common interest (in the early stages of writing this book, I joined one of Ravelry's ever-expanding number of "groups," the Spirituality of Knitting Group).

Ravelry is the creative offspring of a young couple, Jessica and Casey Forbes. Jessica had the inspiration to put on a single site all the information that fiber artists might need: about yarns, patterns, other knitters' and crocheters' projects, fiber arts events, and more; and Casey had the technical know-how to make it happen. In May 2007, they launched the site. Now it is the go-to spot for knitters, crocheters, and spinners around the world—a combined fiber art resource and social networking site. Any member can keep track of her or his own projects, start a group, initiate a discussion thread on a forum, or ask for help with a project or technique.

Knitters love to bond, to share their yarns. But don't we all? Isn't this a basic human need—to share our yarns, our life stories? I believe it is. So does Dr. Melanie C. Reuter, executive director of the Wesley Foundation (United Methodist campus ministry) at the University of Cincinnati. On her wonderfully titled blog *Hands to Soul* (HandsToSoul.wordpress.com), Melanie wrote about "Knitting as a Spiritual Journey" for her May 27, 2008, post:

Years ago, a friend encouraged me to learn to knit. I was reluctant to learn to knit, but once I began, I realized I had embarked on a spiritual journey. Here are some of the things I learned as I began to knit.

On our spiritual journeys, we need companions. It is the connection with others that gets us through the truly difficult times of life. This is true in knitting as well. You can buy instruction books and videos to teach you to knit, but they're not enough; you have to have someone to help you along the way. No matter how good the instructions, eventually you will get to an impasse in your knitting that only another human being can help you through.

We are given this life to share with one another. Knitting can be a means to share our yarns. Knitting can be a spiritual journey; a spiritual journey can bring one into knitting. We are created to be close-knit.

Prayer

Creator of us all,
Knitter of our lives and loves—
We give you thanks for the joys of companionship on our journeys,
For the sharing of patterns and pearls, of yearnings and yarns,
For the friends whose lives are knit into our own.

PATTERNING YOUR PRAYER

Star Felted Coasters

by Lynn Davis and Marilyn Schubert

For the theme of community, coasters are a natural. With these delightful ones (created by the owner and a staff member of Tucson's Kiwi Knitting Company), you can sip drinks as you socialize and knit.

Gauge: 5 stitches and 8 rows = 1 inch in garter stitch.

Yarn: 50 grams of a worsted weight 100 percent wool (must be wool as these coasters will be felted).

Needles: US8 circular (any cord length) and a set of US8 double-pointed needles (dpns).

K = Knit the indicated number of stitches.

K2tog = Knit 2 stitches together.

Slip = Entering stitch as if to purl, simply move stitch from left to right needle.

Make 5 points:

Row 1: Using circular needle, cast on 3 stitches. Knit 1 row.

Row 2: Cast on 1 stitch using Cable Cast-on (described on the next page), knit to last stitch, move working yarn forward and slip last stitch onto right needle.

Rows 3 and 4: Repeat Row 2 (6 stitches).

Row 5: K5, move yarn forward and slip last stitch.

Rows 6–9: Repeat Row 2 (10 stitches).

Rows 10 and 11: Knit all stitches until last stitch; move yarn forward and slip last stitch.

Break yarn and start a new point. You can hold each point separately on the circular needle until you've completed all 5. For 5th point, do not break off yarn.

Make the center of the star:

Round 1: Join the 5 points using double-pointed needles (dpns) by knitting across the first point, then the second, third, until you've knit all stitches on the 5th point. Distribute 16–17 stitches on each of 3 dpns. Place a marker to mark the round (50 stitches).

Round 2: Knit.

Round 3: *K2, K2tog, repeat from * to last 2 stitches, K2 (38 stitches).

Round 4: Knit.

Round 5: *K2, K2tog, repeat from * to last 2 stitches, K2tog (28 stitches).

Round 6: Knit.

Round 7: *K2, K2tog, repeat from * (21 stitches).

Round 8: Knit.

Round 9: *K1, K2tog, repeat from * (14 stitches).

Round 10: Knit.

Round 11: *K1, K2tog, repeat from * to last 2 stitches, K2 (10 stitches).

Round 12: K2tog across the round, binding off as you go.

Make 3–4 more stars for each set of coasters. You can also incorporate contrasting colors or novelty yarns for one or more rounds of the center or rows of the points.

Finishing: Sew in all ends. Place stars in a lingerie bag and wash in smallest possible load using very hot water, a little detergent, and a pair of jeans to help the agitation for 15–20 minutes. (Time for felting varies, so check every 5–8 minutes.) Remove after wash cycle, shape, and allow to air dry. Felting can also be done by hand in a tub of very hot soapy water, rubbing the stars by hand, and alternating a rinse in very cold clean water to increase the felting.

Cable Cast-on: Insert right needle between the first 2 stitches, draw through a loop using the yarn from the ball and slip loop onto left needle by rotating the left needle toward you and down, then up through the loop on the right needle.

FOUR

Knit One, Purl a Pattern

> You can make beauty, and honor this
> beautiful world where we live.
> — Denise Frame Harlan,
> "Spinning a Yarn: or Giving It a Whirl"

The Yarn Is Like My Life

K nitting," Christine Bochen had said at that Yarn Boutique chat, "is both solitary and communal." In chapter 3, I focused on knitting's communal dimension. But now I want to return to the topic of solitary knitting. Chapters 1 and 2 have already suggested some ways that solitary knitting can be spiritually enriching: how knitting can lead one into the special silence that is awareness of Divine Presence; and how knitting can lend itself to the inner repetition of mantras, as we knit words of wisdom into our heart.

Sometimes, though, when I'm knitting alone in the evening, instead of saying a mantra in my mind I enjoy just watching the knitted pattern forming through my fingers. I choose a bit of the yarn to follow as it loops around (like trying to follow the fall of a snowflake or a wave as it rolls toward shore), the old stitch moving into the loop below the right needle, or my working yarn forming the next stitch as I pull the old stitch off of the left needle.

Other knitters who have attended to the patterns formed by their knitting offer reflections on the larger significance of patterning.

Christine's friend Sheila Smyth said to us at the Yarn Boutique discussion, "I like how the yarn is like my life: a single strand winding in and out—creating a pattern."

Sheila's comment set me thinking: all knitting is the creation of patterns, and so is our life. Followers of a religious tradition strive to follow the pattern or path set by a founder or sacred text. Christians have the tradition of *Imitatio Christi*: conforming one's life to the shape of Christ's. Muslims pattern their lives on the life of the Prophet Muhammad. Core to Jewish tradition is following patterns of behavior that are faithful to God's covenantal values of justice and loving-kindness. Buddhists strive to follow the pattern of the Buddha's life and teachings. The Bhagavad Gita offers Hindus the guidance of Krishna as he teaches Arjuna the right path of life.

Many religions speak of following a pathway laid out by transcendent wisdom. I love the line from Psalm 119: "Your word is a lamp to my feet and a light to my path" (v. 105).

But none of this following of pathways and patterns is slavish; always the follower is invited into creativity, into making one's own the pattern offered as model or guide. All religious traditions honor the free choice given to human beings and the invitation to respond creatively to divine guidance.

Pam Henager of Kennewick, Washington, muses on the inventiveness needed to follow patterns in her July 31, 2006, post "The Japanese Sweater as Metaphor" on her blog *Works in Progress*. First, Pam describes the sweater pattern's complexities, with photos of the

pattern graph. To me, the graph looks itself like an overwhelmingly intricate work of art, a graphic design. Then Pam notes:

> One of the neatest things about these Japanese patterns is that the diagram shows how many centimeters wide *each* pattern in the sweater should be. So, I knit a swatch of the center pattern on size 6 needles. It was less than a half a centimeter too wide. Since I liked the look of it, and since I needed to make the sweater a bit bigger anyway, I decided it would be OK like this. I also knit a seed stitch swatch, because I think I'll need to add some extra stitches as well, and the seed stitch panels would be the easiest place to do this. I still have to figure out what effect this might have on my raglan shaping, since I'm not changing the sleeves at all.
>
> I've made copies of the stitch pattern graphs, and then added to it, both by adding copies of more pattern repeats (since the various patterns have different numbers of rows, this should help me keep track of where I am), *and* also by making a mirror image of the graphs so my sweater will be symmetrical.

Finally, Pam reflects on how knitting this sweater relates to her life:

> I think I understand what I need to know to make this sweater. And it's not brain surgery (or heart surgery, for

As you knit a few rows, just notice the pattern taking shape in your hands. Then put your knitting down and reflect on the patterns that you follow in your life.

that matter), so if I'm wrong, I've only wasted some time and some yarn. Nobody will die. But this is how this sweater is like life. There's information on this page and in this book that I don't understand. And not only do I not understand it, I don't actually know what information I'm missing. It could be the secret of life, or of making this sweater perfectly, or it could be some artistic or commercial fluff about the yarn or the pattern. I can't tell. Life's like that sometimes. It would be nice to have all the answers, or even just to know where one is ignorant or wrong. But I'm not God, and I'm not a Japanese knitting designer. I'm just a humble knitter trying to follow along, and make something nice if I can.

Elephants on Parade

The kind of attention that knitting a complicated pattern requires can be meditative in the same way as listening to music can be: when your mind is focused on following the pattern in music, other preoccupations tend to drop away. "The active listening required by classical music," writes composer James MacMillan, "may be said to be analogous to contemplation, meditation, and even prayer. This kind of listening demands our time. The complex, large-scale forms of serious music unfold their narratives with an authority that cannot be hurried."

I experienced something of this when doing my first piece of stranded knitting, a wool hat for my great-nephew's first birthday. I certainly wouldn't call it a "large-scale form": after all, it was only a baby hat. Yet following the pattern's narrative drew me into the unhurried, meditative state that MacMillan describes.

The pattern was called "Elephants on Parade." On a white background, gray-blue elephants circled the hat, big ones below, and smaller ones as the hat decreased in diameter toward the top of the head. Between the rows of elephants were cheery red-checkered rows.

The designer's pattern posed two new challenges for me. The elephants were graphed onto a pattern chart, showing which color to use for which stitch as you moved across the row. I'd never followed a pattern chart before; all my previous knitting projects had verbal instructions. But once I got the hang of following the tiny colored squares, I gained confidence in this visual way of following a pattern.

The second new challenge was the stranded knitting, which involved carrying two different color yarns across the row, the unused color carried as a loose strand behind the color in use. I hadn't yet learned about holding one strand in each hand, a technique I've since come to love. So while knitting two gray-blue stitches for the elephant's rear leg, I let the white yarn hang loose in the back, then picked it up to create the space between the elephant's legs, leaving the gray-blue yarn loose; then for the front leg's two gray-blue stitches, did the reverse.

Once I figured out how to keep these two colors of yarn from getting tangled, I relaxed into the focused concentration that following this pattern required. I did have to focus; no daydreaming here! But as I saw the little elephants take shape in my hands, I felt the joy of creative accomplishment. It seemed almost miraculous: how these little creatures could come to a kind of life from two strands of yarn.

I remembered (not *while* knitting, since during the process my mind had to stay fixed on the creative present, but when I'd rest between rows to gaze with fulfillment at the work) how the figure of Wisdom speaks about creativity in the Bible's book of Proverbs. She, Wisdom, was created by God, she says, "at the beginning of his work," so that she was present to witness his creation of our universe. "When he established the heavens, I was there, when he drew a circle on the face of the deep, . . . when he assigned to the sea its limit, . . . when he marked out the foundations of the earth." As God molded these forms of heaven, seas, and earth, Wisdom watched in joy and even, she suggests, participated in the creative work: "then I was beside him, like a master worker; and I was daily his delight, rejoicing before him always, rejoicing in his inhabited world and delighting in the human race" (Prov. 8:27–31).

Sharing in the creativity of the designer of "Elephants on Parade" seemed to me at least a bit like Wisdom's sharing in God's creative work: a designer creates the original pattern; but "beside" the designer is the one who delights in helping bring the pattern into being.

Wisdom's rejoicing as she shared in the divine creativity was, as I imagine it, a *meditative* joy. Being "there" as God "established" heaven, earth, and humankind would be a witnessing in wonder. This would be a meditative experience beyond that of listening to music, beyond focusing the mind on following the pattern. Wisdom—and a knitter following the designer's knitting pattern—is "following" the pattern in a medium that helps bring the pattern into being. The musical analogy here would be to the performer's art: the musician follows the composer's pattern and in doing so with attentive creative energy, brings the composer's design to life anew with each performance.

And so with following a complex pattern in knitting: it is meditative, but a dynamic, creative meditation.

Creator of our cosmos,
Designer of our days—
May we dance before you as Wisdom danced at your creation
of the world.
May we perform your works in a way that gives you pleasure,
That lightens the load of our fellow creatures,
That pours on them a portion of your Love.

Magical Power

Sharah Blankenship contacted me after I'd announced to my knitting guild that I welcomed anyone's thoughts on how knitting intersected with spirituality in their lives. We met at a local coffee shop, and Sharah told me her story. She is a young wife, active in her church, and she brimmed over with joy as she recounted what struck me as a unique perspective on the spiritual dimension of knitting's creativity.

My grandma died when I was seven. She was our knitter. She made sweaters for birthdays and Christmases. She knit all our stuff. She was Irish and loved fairy tales.

I loved the magic of them. I've been thinking especially about the fairy tale called *The Wild Swans* by Hans Christian Anderson because for me now it's about the power of knitting, of creativity. In a nutshell, the plot is that a girl has seven brothers, who are turned into swans by an evil stepmother. They can be freed only if their sister spins and knits a shirt for each of them, while remaining completely silent. The story indicates weaving and sewing, but knitting would be more logical a craft for making shirts. She goes through lots of typical fairy-tale trials, but finally she does manage to make the shirts and free her brothers—except she doesn't quite finish the final shirt, so one brother remains with one arm as a swan's. What impacted me as a child about this story is the *power of creativity*. Its magical power.

My mom sewed. She didn't knit. But I wanted to knit, and I think it is because of fairy tales like this one and their association with my grandma, who probably told me a few and who was a knitter. An aunt taught me to knit when I was about nine. But I didn't really get into it until college, when I began knitting like crazy. And I haven't stopped.

As a Christian, I wonder: does the Lord imbue our creative work with a special power—as if the Holy Spirit gets knit into a shawl I'm making, or into whatever I'm knitting? I think of it like an invisible thread, and as I knit, that invisible thread is knitted into the items I make for the people that I love. I think that this is possible even when I am not consciously praying over a piece. I feel like the love I have for the person I am making it for will shine through to be evident. Having joined the Prayer Shawl ministry at my mom's church, I see this even more. The Holy Spirit, known as the Comforter, seems to imbue the act of knitting with comfort and sometimes healing—even if it is emotional rather than spiritual. And that to me seems magical, like the girl making sweaters for her brothers in order to turn them back into men. Her silence was a part of that, her contemplation and love.

I find much in Sharah's reflections to ponder. The contemplative dimension of knitting's healing power. The striking image of the Holy Spirit as an invisible thread knitting comfort into the knitter's work. Knitting's creativity as a kind of magic.

Sharah's sense of knitting's magical power recalled for me Deborah Bergman's account of the Navajo creation story in her book *The Knitting Goddess*. In this book, Bergman chooses ten archetypal female figures from various cultures and finds in their stories insights into the power of creating and patterning—whether with thread, yarn, or any other fiber. For the Navajo, it was Grandmother Spider who was instrumental in creating the world, teaching her people "how to physically create form, pattern, structure, and symbolism." Bergman sees Grandmother Spider as "a testament to the power of the small, and

Meditation

As you knit, what happens if you think of your knitting as magical? Or as sacred? Do you sense a creative power at work through you while you knit?

the healing potential of patterning." And this, Bergman speculates, is perhaps "part of the magic that still invites women, and men, to pick up yarn and needles at a moment of sacred awkwardness in their lives."

I Have a Picture in My Head

My knitting mentor and friend Tina Turner was chatting with me in her home about her delight in creating patterns. "When I design something new, I do it on my needles as I go along. I like to look at the stitches and see what patterns they're forming, then decide how to go from there."

Like any artist, I thought. Like anyone, that is, who puts to use the creativity that seems inherent in human nature. As poet and essayist Luci Shaw says,

> Though we cannot produce something out of nothing, as God did, we can combine the elements and forms available to us in striking and original ways that arise out of the unique human ability (designed and built into us by God) to imagine, to see *pictures in our heads* . . . to hear sounds and rhythms and recognize patterns and to translate them into forms that will strike a chord in the hearts of other human beings.

In that group discussion at Yarn Boutique on what draws us all to knitting and what it means in our lives, Tina unknowingly echoed one of Luci's phrases. We were talking about creativity in relation to following patterns, and Tina told us how creativity works for her:

I have a picture in my head of what I want to make. I look
for the picture in my head, and then I knit. I have to make
the picture emerge from my head into a knitted work.
One day I had a beautiful yarn and I wondered what I'd
do with it. I woke up at 7 AM suddenly knowing what I'd
do. I ran right downstairs to start it even though it was
Sunday morning and I could have stayed in bed.

Tina's daughter Natasha was also at the discussion. A college student and avid knitter as well as a musician, Natasha saw an analogy
between her two creative media: "I had a jazz teacher in high school.
He wanted me to play jazz on my flute, but I resisted at first. Then I
tried it and loved it. He used to say 'sound plus feel equals music.' I
see the equation in knitting. It's not the needles and the yarn, but what
happens when you do it."

This comment stimulated Meghan, a church organist, to chime
in: "Creativity requires freedom—for composing music or for knitting. I think of freedom and limits. You have a form and a style, then
you bring in ideas of your own. So with knitting, it isn't just about a
pattern; I have to connect the work somehow with myself."

Valerie, another knitter who has become a close friend through
our knitting together, told us how her work connects with—and
comes out of—herself. "I was taking a workshop in Tacoma with
designer Kathryn Alexander. Someone asked me what I was making.
I said, 'It hasn't decided yet.'" As Val spoke, she continued knitting
on a tiny sweater for her baby grandson. "On this sweater for Oscar,

I won't decide for a long time which animal I'll knit into the front piece. Sometimes I knit things without knowing what the shape will be. Color is what keeps me going; I choose colors I love to work with together, then I design as I go."

Sheila Smyth went home from our discussion and told her husband, Mike Heberger, about it. The next day I got an email from Mike full of analogies between knitting and what he experiences in his hobby of woodworking. On following one's creative impulse, he wrote: "There is great joy to planning the next project and the wood to use—and then *changing* it because of better wood, or cost, or availability."

With all this energizing talk of creativity buzzing in my mind, I found online the marvelously creative group of fiber artists in Lancashire, England, called ArtYarn (artyarn.blogspot.com). "ArtYarn," they write, "view knitting and crochet as an opportunity for individual creative expression and at the same time explore the medium as a way to make art accessible through participatory making." Their specialty is public knitting projects or "outdoor installations" that they call "yarn bombing"—like wrapping a city tree trunk or street sign in brightly multicolored knitting. Coming across these wildly exuberant fiber creations would bring a smile, I'd think, to anyone's ordinary day.

Speaking of the joy of creativity, knitter Denise Frame Harlan of Gloucester, Massachusetts, who also spins her own yarn, writes in her online article "Spinning a Yarn: or Giving It a Whirl":

This is my legacy to my children and their friends: you can make things yourself, things more precious than you can buy. You can make beauty, and honor this beautiful world where we live. Quality materials make all the difference. You can see what happens when this color mixes with that. It's an experiment. Spinning, knitting, weaving, painting, stitching—this list is just the beginning. Give it a whirl. Mama's family makes things that make them happy.

I Can See Myself Taking Shape

Luci Shaw is not only a poet and essayist; she is also a long-time knitter. Luci sent me a journal entry where she muses on knitting patterns as a metaphor for her life. Dated January 2, 1987, the entry begins:

I'm making some progress at last on my new project—the sweater I promised to knit for my friend Candace. She paid a lot for the yarn, and I must admit it is a joy to work with—dark charcoal gray with slate blue and black fibers, and flecks of red and blue and green. It is heavy—that is, it has heft; it feels substantial as it inches through my fingers onto the needles.

The pattern is a continental one translated, very badly, from Italian to English, which makes it ambiguous and confusing. Added to that, the yarn shop owner made some adjustments for this particular yarn, which is not the yarn the pattern calls for. The woman's scribblings also feel like a foreign language, too indistinct to read

When you knit, how do you "connect the work with yourself," as Meghan put it? Is it through the colors or yarn texture that you choose? Through changes, small or large, that you make to a designer's pattern? Through designing your pattern as you go? Does your sense of creativity connect you to God?

easily. It's incomplete as well—she doesn't follow through consistently, leaving me with a lot of guesswork.

What this means is that I end up being my own designer. . . .

The journal entry then turns quietly into a reflection on knitting one's life, Luci's words gliding so smoothly into this reflection that most of the paragraph refers at once to both literal and metaphorical knitting:

I am feeling, in the rough texture of the years as the garment grows in my hands, and from the repetitious click of the metal needles, what it is like, also, to knit a life. How experimental it is. How the instructions are not always intelligible and often make no sense until I knit them into reality, doing it over and over until it's right. How when I first start a pattern I can't discern the effect I'm working toward, but I follow the general idea anyway and see what happens, adapting as necessary, and finally something interesting and warm and beautiful takes shape under my fingers.

Luci then goes on, true poet that she is, to hold and work simultaneously these two strands: her experience of actual knitting patterns and her life's experimental patterning:

A slow process, stitch added to stitch, and row to row, the work picked up and put down at odd moments the way one adds to one's own life by fits and starts. Single as I am, widowed after 33 years of marriage, I know that

I'm knitting a new project, a major one, as big as this long, bulky jacket for Candy—no incidental sock or mitten. For all my wedded years I've knitted traditional Aran fisherman sweaters—complex, certainly, with convoluted cables and ribs and popcorns and honeycombs and mosses and seed stitches, but recognizable within their genre. But this pattern is all new, the style unique. There will be no other sweater just like this, and though I have a pattern of sorts, my own trial and error and decision and will shape it into my own creation. I don't know yet what it will look like, finished. But the effort *feels* infinitely worthwhile.

Finally, she lets the metaphor of life as knitting finish solidly on its own:

I am both knitter and knitted one. I can see myself taking shape, all my yarns and fibers looped in rows that hold together and capture within them the tiny pockets of air that insulate and comfort the body—the air is part of the pattern, plained and pearled into the pieces. Knitted stitch by stitch, hour by hour, it will take all of the years of my life to complete. O my Lord, I hope it looks good when it's done—a seamless garment.

True poet and truly faith-filled person, Luci has found her musings on her knitted life moving naturally into that closing prayer.

And don't we all hope that our life looks good when it's done? That our rows looped over the years will somehow be patterned into a work of warmth and beauty?

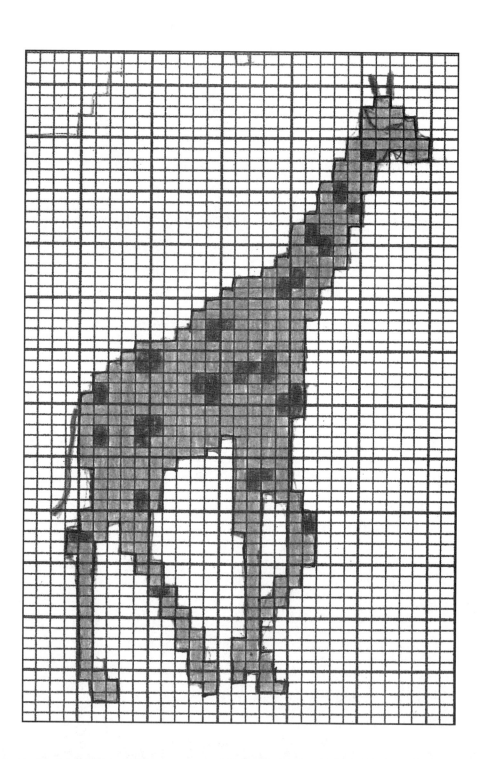

PATTERNING YOUR PRAYER
Intarsia Giraffe
by Valerie McPherson

Intarsia is a method of knitting a colored shape into your work. Tutorials are available online. Designer Valerie McPherson offers these comments on her creative process:

"When I sit down to knit, I like to relax and let the fiber take me where it will.

"With a piece like this, of course I graphed the giraffe before beginning. If you have any hesitations about tackling intarsia, you can simply knit the giraffe without the spots and later embroider them using duplicate stitch [tutorials also available online].

"When I do intarsia, I prefer to look at the public side of the garment. So I knit backward on the purl rows. That way I don't have to reverse the image in my mind as I work. Not for everybody, but soothing for me."

Oscar's Cardigan

The giraffe is one of several animals Valerie knit into a cardigan for her grandson Oscar. This giraffe was placed on the right front panel, so the giraffe looked toward the center buttons and toward him. At a gauge of 5.5 stitches per 1" and 7.5 rows per 1", Oscar's giraffe is 4.9" x 7.7" and fits easily on a small sweater.

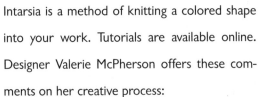

Gauge matters:

Using the same graph, the giraffe can be knit at a fine gauge for a baby sweater.

Or, at a larger gauge, it can be the central design on the front or back of a sweater.

Some gauge options are:

Lightweight yarn	8 stitches per 1" x 8.5 rows per 1"	yields a giraffe 3.25" x 6.7"
Baby weight yarn	6.5 stitches per 1" x 8.5 rows per 1"	yields a giraffe 4" x 7"
Heavier worsted yarn	4.5 stitches per 1" x 6 rows per 1"	yields a giraffe 6" x 9.6"

FIVE

Knit One, Purl the Pain

> Knitting soothes the troubled spirit, and it
> doesn't hurt the untroubled spirit either.
> — Elizabeth Zimmermann,
> *Knitting Without Tears*

Knitting Through Trauma

Though I've been knitting since I was six years old, I'm not
a regular knitter. I don't always have a project going. But
some years ago, when my daughter Tara was a teenager,
she had a terribly troubled time and went off the rails.
She disappeared from home. For several months I lived in
agony, not knowing where she was, whether she was safe
or not. I knew that if I hired a detective to trace her, that
would only antagonize her further. So I lived with this
constant agonizing fear for her.

Halifax resident Pat was telling me this harrowing story over the
phone. My sister in Canada had put us in touch when I was beginning
to write this book. Pat went on:

Something moved me to begin knitting an afghan for Tara.
For my own sanity, I had to do *something* for her since she

wouldn't accept my direct help. I had a job to support myself, so I didn't have lots of time to knit. But every night at bedtime, I'd knit one row of the afghan. I wasn't a religious person at the time, but I felt each stitch as a prayer for her safety. Blankets are to wrap up in, to be protected by. So I could focus my concentration on creating something that could literally protect her. I saw it as a security blanket.

Eventually Tara came home, but I could never face that blanket again, though it remained unfinished. Picking up the project would have been picking up again that dreadful time that I then needed to leave behind.

But about ten years later, Tara—by then doing fine on her own as a young adult living in western Canada—came home for a family event. I asked her to unravel the unfinished afghan with me, so that I could use the wool to make a sweater for her. I needed this ritual with her, and she agreed to do it with me. Together we unraveled the afghan, so that symbolically we were unraveling that terrible time in our lives. We were undoing the hard time and re-balling it to create something anew.

Later in our phone conversation, Pat said, "Knitting is such a powerful metaphor. And ripping out, unraveling: I wish we could do this in life." Yet, in the unraveling ritual she'd devised with her daughter, she had indeed to some extent unraveled that terrible piece of their lives.

Pat's experience has given me a way to think about what it might mean to "knit through" a trauma. I haven't suffered anything like Pat's agony when her daughter ran away. But once knitting helped me through a heartbreak. My husband and I are very close with a young couple whom we've known since their childhoods. Though they live out of town, we used to visit each other often. On one of our visits to their home, they told us they were divorcing. We were devastated for them both. During the trip home, I'd planned to continue a knitting project I was doing for them: scarves for their Christmas gifts. I said to my husband, "I'm not sure I want to finish this project; it will continually remind me of their brokenness." But George said, "No, you must do the knitting—knit *through* the pain, the grief, the loss."

Back at home later that week, while knitting on their scarves, I heard well up in me the beginning of Psalm 130: "Out of the depths I cry to you, O Lord." I'd long ago learned this psalm by heart, so *from* my heart the line could naturally rise when needed. Its rhythm matched the rhythm of my stitches as I knit along each row. This silent repetition of the line knit the psalmist's pained cry deeper into my being, at the same time as the pain somehow passed through the knitting.

The pain for my young friends didn't disappear. But in creating something for them with my needles, something warm and comforting, I—like Pat knitting her daughter a security blanket—was transforming

Have you ever "knit
through" a trauma—or used
another creative craft to
help you through? If so,
meditate with the memory.
How do you think the
creative work of your hands
helped heal your inner
being?

at least a bit of my suffering into an object that might console both myself and my dear friends.

Knitting Through Illness

When I was hospitalized with a life-threatening case of legionellosis, all I could do was knit. My mind couldn't focus on reading or even watching films, but the movement of the yarn through my hands focused my attention and got me through a month-long illness with a sense of minute-by-minute creative healing and hope.

One knitting experience in the hospital stands out for me and still makes me smile. The back of my right hand was hooked up to an IV line for a three-hour blood transfusion. Naturally, I spent the hours knitting. My project at the time was a two-color slip-stitch pattern, which alternated the yarns after every two rows. So from my hands there were dangling a sage-green yarn, a sky-blue yarn, and the transparent plastic IV line running red blood through it. After about an hour, I put down my knitting needles to rest a bit, and I noticed that the blue yarn had gotten tangled around the IV line—evidently as I'd switched back and forth between the two balls of yarn. I tried to untangle the blue yarn from the blood-red plastic tubing, but it was impossible. I saw that there would be no way to separate them until the transfusion was done and the IV line removed from the back of my hand.

I knit comfortably on, enjoying this new connection of knitting to my very life's blood. Looking down at the (now) three strands of color intertwined as I knit—the blue, the green, and the red—I felt a rush of gratitude that life-saving blood was entering my body, interwoven with my knitting. Because knitting had become for me life-saving in its own way. Not literally, of course. But engaging my hands and my mind in this creative work was keeping me calmly focused—and even peacefully happy—throughout this otherwise scary and physically uncomfortable illness.

Author Betsy Greer, in *Knitting for Good*, reports on scientific evidence that an absorbing activity like knitting can actually reduce pain by distracting the brain from its pain signals. And Greer highlights the website stitchlinks.com, set up in 2003 by Betsan Corkhill, a Bath, England, resident who believes that the medical profession should pay more attention to the healing potential of knitting and other needlework. Corkhill has been collecting on her site the stories of people who have been helped through physical pain, depression, and other illness by needlework. Meanwhile, she continues to advocate with the medical profession, and on her blog for April 17, 2010, she exuberantly reports a breakthrough:

My visit to the British Pain Society's Annual Scientific Meeting in Manchester last week was a *huge* success. After four years of laying the foundations, it seems like we can finally start building upwards! I met lots of healthcare professionals who are really keen to incorporate knitting and knitting groups into their pain management tool boxes. Many commented that they thought we were on to something really important so we're moving into a really exciting stage.

So the medical profession is starting to recognize what knitters have long since discovered for themselves. Back at my hometown yarn store's discussion about knitting's meaning in our lives, Sheila Smyth told us:

Five years ago, I had thyroid cancer. I was having radiation therapy for it and had to be isolated in the hospital and off of my regular thyroid meds. I was knitting a muff. It helped me stay sane during the radiation. But something wasn't going right with the muff. I wasn't finishing it. Then I realized that it was because of those missed medications that I was going so slowly—with everything. But knitting has always been there for me when I needed it.

Sheila's friend Christine added: "I remember, Sheila, when you and I were waiting for news from your doctor about the results of a biopsy. We were in a yarn shop when the doctor called! That's the best place to hear news like that."

Knitting Comfort

When Laurie introduced herself at the start of our discussion at Yarn Boutique, she told us about sitting with her aunt, cousins, and sisters around her mother's deathbed.

When my mom was dying in hospice, she heard me talking with a cousin about someone who wanted to knit. We heard my mom trying to say something. Finally we figured out that she was muttering "Get the book, get the book." She meant her book about knitting. All of us found comfort in knitting around her as she lay dying. She had started to make a quilt before she got sick. We girls finished it later; the quilt was on her bed the night she died. We women in the extended family still get together to knit a couple times a year. Each of us brings a project we're doing, and we just knit together and chat and deepen our bonds.

For Laurie and her extended family, knitting reinforces interconnections in the way we saw in chapter 3: relations are more deeply interwoven as the needles click along. But there's the added comfort, too, of knitting at the bedside of a loved one. Knitting's power to calm the inner spirit comes to our aid in the anxious uncertainty of tending a loved one who is gravely ill.

Valerie recounted her own experience in response to Laurie's. "My daughter once had to go to the hospital. I went with her, calling a friend who thought I wanted her to bring clothes. But what I asked for was yarn, for a *complicated* project. I needed the complexity to focus my attention away from my anxiety and fear for my daughter."

Leslie concurred: "Once I had to help my sister who was sick in the hospital out of town. I found when I arrived that I hadn't packed enough clothes—but I *had* brought my yarn." And this set off a quick exchange among everyone:

"Odd that they don't have yarn in hospital gift shops."

"But they couldn't carry all the types of yarn."

"That wouldn't matter."

"Sometimes you just need to knit, and you don't care what the yarn is. You can knit it on chopsticks or pencils if you have to."

Sometimes you just need to knit. And by a sickbed is one of those times. Another is when unspoken comfort needs to be offered to someone who is suffering—whether from news of a cancer diagnosis, or anxiety about a son in the military overseas, or loss of a close friend or spouse. Meghan, along with other members of her knitting group, had been able to offer this comfort:

It's hard to see someone you love suffering. But being in a knitting group with that person is good. You don't have the pressure of having to *say* something to the person. You can just *be* together. It's solidarity. You can't *help*, but you can *be together*, just moving your hands even if you can't talk—because talk is too hard.

Sue added, with a sort of blessing to Meghan's words, "That's knitting as communion. Communion as community."

Knitting Through Grief

Whenever I interviewed any knitter for this book, she would nearly always start—without my asking—by telling me how she first began to knit. Then pretty soon she'd move into what was really on her mind: what knitting had meant and continued to mean in her life. So it was with Becky White.

After we'd gotten comfortably seated on Becky's living room couch, she began:

My aunt taught me when I was a child—somewhere around nine to twelve years old. Then I didn't do it much. In the 1970s, crochet was all the craze—those granny afghans—and I did some of that. But I was busy working as a teacher, and then in the mid-80s I went back to grad school in social work. Then I worked as a social worker for kids with special emotional problems. So I had no time to knit.

But out of nowhere in 2004, her husband was diagnosed with cancer. He died three and a half months later.

Then the very next January, my mother was found to have pancreatic cancer. She died in 2005. My father had serious dementia, so on my mother's death he had to be moved to assisted living. Losing both my husband and mother

within a year was hard. I hadn't been able to have a grieving process for my husband, because I'd had to plunge
right into my parents' needs.

Knitting had become popular again—I wonder when
exactly that was? During this double grieving time, I
re-taught myself to knit. I'd go to Michael's (the craft store
with inexpensive yarns) and buy lots of novelty yarns. I'd
knit them into scarves. The repetitive motion of basic stitch
patterns was just what I needed. I'd give the scarves to
women at my dad's assisted living center. He died in 2007.

Then my brother died suddenly of a massive heart
attack. I joined a grief support group. But I also kept
knitting: the repetitive motion of the scarves became a
calming meditation. Gradually I realized that my Higher
Power had knit me back together.

Becky paused thoughtfully. Then she summed up how knitting
had gradually healed her grief:

While knitting those scarves, I started choosing more complex patterns and when I'd hit a hard spot, I'd reach out to
people to help me. This pulled me out of the isolation of my
grief. I'd been staying home a lot, and I needed to get out
and start mixing with people. Knitting became my vehicle for
this reconnection with life. It became a way of sitting with
people and just *being* with them.

Becky's transformative experience—of knitting through and eventually out of grief—is not unique. Of course, the details of her grace-filled story are unique. But knitters everywhere seek out each other in times of grief. Ravelry has more than half a dozen different support groups for knitters who are suffering a grief: from divorce, miscarriage, or the death of a child or a spouse or a parent.

Sometimes our life just breaks apart. It can be gradual; it can be sudden. Pittsburgh pastor M. Craig Barnes writes of visiting an elderly nursing home resident who tearfully told him, "You lose life in pieces. And then one day you find yourself here, and you have a lot of time to wonder: where did it all go?" The resident's agonized experience was of *gradual* loss: "losing life in pieces." Poet Naomi Shihab Nye, in her poem "Breaking My Favorite Bowl," finds an image for *sudden* loss: when an ordinary afternoon, like a ceramic bowl slipped from her hands, will "thud unexpectedly" as it shatters on the floor.

Yet knitters testify that knitting somehow draws life back together, recovers the lost pieces one stitch at a time. I don't want to make this sound facile: the loss remains. But there is another strand of wholeness mysteriously running through it.

As Becky White put it: "Knitting made me a person who could go out and do things, instead of getting stuck in isolated depression. I love that it was through the creative process that you can be knit back together."

Meditation

At times when your life has broken apart, have you found a means for putting it back together? For Becky, it was both the craft and the communal dimension of knitting that stitched her back together, reconnected her with life. Reflect on the life-affirming power of this mysterious, marvelous conjunction of craft and community.

Knitting Through Public Pain

"Knitters yearn for yarn and companionship in a world of uncertainty." This was the title of an article in *USA Today*'s weekend edition of April 7, 2002. The article opens by profiling a group of young adults who gathered to knit on the Tuesday evening exactly a week after the violent events of September 11, 2001.

They gathered at their local yarn shop, La Knitterie Parisienne in Los Angeles. "They needed to get away from the television and just to talk to each other," owner Edith Eig told *USA Today*. To talk and to knit: the inner calm and interpersonal bonding that knitting can facilitate were needed especially in the aftermath of the country's dreadful loss.

And immediately, knitting's impulse toward outreach also came into play. That very night, the group of knitters consoling one another felt moved to begin knitting blankets for their local fire department— inspired by the heroic role of New York City's firefighters in response to the terrorist attacks on the World Trade Center.

I myself wasn't yet a knitter at that time. But my own need after September 11th was to put myself in the presence of creativity, of art. I needed the affirmation of life that creativity represents. So I went to a chamber music concert that very Sunday, and to my city's art museum throughout the week. I can easily relate, therefore, to the words quoted in a companion piece to this *USA Today* article. The speaker was Elizabeth Ross Balderston, the great-great-great-great-granddaughter of Betsy Ross, who is credited with sewing the first

American flag in 1776. "What I've come to realize," Balderston said, "is that all of us are artists in our own ways, and when life doesn't seem to make any sense at all, art helps to make the world whole."

On the other side of the globe, knitter Kathryn Gunn was moved by the same conviction—that art helps to make the world whole—in her response to September 11th. A resident of Adelaide, Australia, Kathryn describes her inspired project in a September 19, 2001, email to the website KnittingUniverse.com. Her subject heading is "extraordinary KIPping journey." (KIP is the knitters' acronym for the intentional activity of Knitting in Public.)

Dear Knitf(r)iends

Yesterday I had occasion to take two long journeys on Adelaide's public transport. As usual I was KIPping but this time on one of the journeys a woman opposite me asked what I was making and I was able to tell her "a peace blanket" and explained what the symbols and words meant. [The words meant "peace" in various languages.] Her face lit up so I held out the knitting and asked, "Would you like to add a couple of stitches for peace?" So, she took the knitting and did just that, then she passed it to the woman across the aisle from her and she passed it on . . . and everyone in the bus who could knit added a stitch or two if the person next to them could not knit and when I reached my destination the driver stopped the bus and held out his hand and added a stitch or two as well.

Clearly everyone on that bus also felt at some deep level that this spontaneous communal art project could somehow "help make the world whole."

Spreading peace through the click of your needles, sending hope for the world's hurts through the work of one's hands—Susan Mark Landis describes her own discovery of this healing truth. In an article called "Knit One, Pray One," on the Mennonite e-zine site *PeaceSigns*, Susan recalls her distress after returning home to Ohio after a stint in Palestine with the Mennonite Central Committee and Christian Peacemaker Teams. (CPTs go to places of conflict throughout the world and try simply to be a nonviolent, healing presence there.) On first returning home, she writes:

> I found myself agitated. At the end of many days, all I had to show was a long list of emails in my Sent file, dirty dishes and a disparaging spirit. I had not centered well during the trip. I had been too noisy and talkative. To my surprise, the remedy I discovered was knitting. Even completing a few rows an evening might have visible results over time, I figured. . . .

She talks next about honing her knitting skills, making scarves for CPT members. And then:

We're to the inevitable question—what does knitting have to do with peacemaking? And likely the answers are quite obvious. Knitting helps me center and calm and think, and I am finally proficient enough that I can also pray as I knit. . . . Sitting at a computer all day can drain the spirit. Creating something visible for someone I care about is rejuvenating. I can't fix the problems the CPTers in Hebron face as they work, but I am sending them a shawl over which I've prayed, and others have prayed, so they can visualize and be wrapped in the care that folks around the world offer them.

PATTERNING YOUR PRAYER

Ruffled Comfort

by Tina Turner

This cozy pillow, with its cheery ruffle on the front side, makes a comforting gift to anyone suffering emotional or physical pain.

Abbreviation: M1 = Make one extra stitch by inserting left needle front to back beneath running thread, then knit into the back of this loop.

Gauge: 22 stitches = 4"
Sock weight yarn, 2 colors. MC (Main Color): 600 yds; CC (Contrast Color): 200 yds.

Yarn used in sample:
Periwinkle Sheep Watercolor II Sock Yarn. Colorways: Main Color deep red-purple; Contrast Color light purple. You can use any two strongly contrasting complementary colors.

Needles: US5 or 6, 16–24" circular needle, or size to obtain gauge.
14" x 14" or 16" x 16" pillow form.

Pattern:
With MC, cast on 168 stitches. Join in the round, being careful not to twist stitches. Add marker to show beginning of round.

MC stripe: Knit in stockinette stitch for 3.5".

CC Stripe: See description below.

Alternate between these two stripes until you have 4 in MC and 3 in CC. Bind off, and sew seam for top of pillow. Add ruffle to each CC stripe. Insert pillow form and sew up bottom. If using 16" x 16" pillow form, the cover will be slightly stretched. Snuggle up!

CC Stripe: With CC purl first 84 stitches, knit next 84 stitches. Then knit in stockinette stitch for 3 more rows. (Since you're working in the round, this means knitting all stitches). You'll have 4 rows in CC, which will be about ½" wide.

Ruffle: Turn pillow upside down with purl stitches on top of CC row. Using MC, pick up and knit every MC purl bump by inserting needle from bottom of bump to top. Purl one row, knit one row, then purl 3rd row. On 4th row: *K2, M1*, repeat between *s to end of row, end with K2. Repeat these 4 rows once more. Purl 1 row in MC. Using CC, knit for 2 rows, then bind off loosely in knit.

SIX

Knit Two, Purl a Prayer

Good God!   Help me see that these

Guide me through the   annoyances:

knots,   knotted emotions,

kinks,   kinked plans,

dropped stitches,   dropped dreams,

split yarn,   split relationships,

shredded fringe,   shredded hopes,

dye lot mismatches,   mismatched friendships,

pattern mistakes,   mistaken assumptions,

errors,   errant goals

and the myriad other "issues"   are actually metaphors of life!

that get in the way of my centeredness!

—Janet Bristow, "Good God!" shawlministry.com

Praying with Your Hands

If this book were a piece of knitting, I might say that now I'm ready to join the work in the round. I'm coming back, that is, to pick up the thread of chapter 1: the motif of prayerful knitting. This topic has run like the yarn of a background motif through the whole work, of course. But now I'm going to bring it forward again as the central theme to follow through this final section of the book.

Why do we knit? How is it prayerful? What does this work of our hands do for our whole body, mind, and spirit? Everything in the book so far has touched on these core questions. Now I want to join together these disparate comments—along with some new threads of thought that complete the larger pattern.

We'll review how it is that knitting can calm one's whole being; we'll consider whether mistakes in knitting can be a spiritual experience; we'll close with a return to prayer shawl knitting, with which the book began. But first, some reflections on knitting as the work of our hands.

Making lovely things with our hands is a spiritual activity. The fourth-century BC Taoist philosopher Chuang Tzu tells of a woodcarver who was commissioned by the prince to make a bell stand. The woodcarver first fasted for days until all thoughts of the court and its pomp had disappeared, leaving him freed from worldly ambition. Then he went into the forest until just the right tree appeared before him; he envisioned the bell stand within the tree. "All I had to do was to put forth my hand and begin." The prince was delighted with the finished bell stand, sure that only the spirits could have made it.

The spirituality of creating with one's hands permeates the Bible as well. The psalms frequently extol God's creativity through the image of divine hands. Psalm 8 exclaims to God with awe: "When I look at your heavens, the work of your fingers, the moon and the stars that you have established. . . ." Psalm 92 chimes in: "At the works of your hands I sing for joy." Further, the psalms express gratitude that the power of God's hands can be humankind's saving grace: "You stretch out your hand," sings Psalm 138, "and your right hand delivers me."

And so, naturally, it is with the image of hands that the psalmist prays for the success of our own endeavors. "O prosper the work of our hands," is the plea of Psalm 90 to the divine power whose own hands create and sustain all our good.

Blogger Dyana Herron reflects on our spiritual need to create with our hands. "A few weeks ago I realized that for a long time now I haven't *made* anything. This isn't to say I have not been involved in creative activities—I write poems, and essays, and very engaging emails. But other than making dinner, I take no physical raw materials and turn them into another object of beauty and functionality. It is, I think, a void in my life."

And why this sense of void when she isn't making something lovely with her hands? Herron explores the question and concludes that "craft provides power—the power to make what you like and perhaps can't find elsewhere, the power to choose your own materials, the power to be more than what you are at your nine-to-five. And the power to realize an important part of your humanity—the capacity to make."

Making is part of the essence of our humanity. So of course we pray, "Prosper the work of our hands."

Knitter Kat Welsh applies this truth, this deep human need, to knitting. In her 2003 article "Knitting Yourself Together" for the online magazine knitty.com, she writes: "Think for a moment about what

Reflect on why, from the time our children can use their hands, we begin teaching them to make things. Both Dyana and Kat suggest that this is a spiritual activity we are teaching our children, although we don't usually think of it that way.

is happening in the actual, physical process of knitting. The knitter takes a strand of yarn and manipulates it, as if by magic, into a piece of cloth with shape and texture. From what is basically a piece of string, using only a few sticks, comes an *object*, a real thing of warmth and beauty." Kat continues: "Knitting isn't really magic, though. And this is the most important part. This amazing transformation of some raw materials into a useful, beautiful, and unique knitted object is done *with the knitter's own hands*. When your project is done, you can show it to the people around you and tell them 'I made this.' That alone is extremely empowering."

Kat's reflections are in response to a question she posed earlier in her article: "Why is knitting so particularly suited to soothing away problems and bringing peace?" It's the question we'll continue to explore in the following section.

Instead of Shredding Styrofoam Cups

"For me, knitting means to relax. It's contemplative. I'm Jewish, though I don't practice the rituals of the religion and don't think of myself as a spiritual person. It's knitting that affords me the opportunity to meditate." A knitter since childhood, seventy-two-year-old Rollie Abkowitz told me this on the phone, as we chatted about what knitting has meant in her life.

In chapters 1 and 2, we talked about knitting's contemplative dimension—which Rollie had discovered for herself over the years. In chapter 5, we talked about knitting's power to soothe the spirit during times of illness or grief. Now I want to focus on knitters' experience of finding that knitting relieves the stress of everyday life.

The knitters at Rochester's Yarn Boutique who gathered to share what knitting means in their lives quickly moved into the topic of relieving stress. Natasha, the college student, told us that when she'd had tendonitis recently, she couldn't knit. "I'm calm right now because at least I can begin to knit again—on big needles. I never knew the calming effect knitting had because I was just knitting continuously. It was when I *couldn't* knit that I realized how much it is a stress-reliever, how much it calms me."

Leslie Shroyer responded with a wry grin: "I knit because I don't smoke. I knit instead of shredding Styrofoam cups."

A Ravelry member from Cologne, Germany, whose user name is Sevenseas, picked up a thread I'd begun about the topic of this book and posted her thoughts about knitting's spirituality. She had been practicing various forms of meditation, she said, and all of it was enriching and useful. "But when I crochet and knit, I feel that all my experiences, knowledge, emotions, and everything I learned on my way are 'put' together to a whole. Everything seems to blend in and I am in a much more calm and serene state than during any other practice. But how it works? I don't know. . . ."

How *does* it work? I asked Dr. Brigid Connolly, a Tucson psychiatrist. Brigid is a knitter and has chosen to spend her Saturdays as a staff member of Kiwi Knitting Company. Although this isn't a usual combination of professions, she loves the mix. "A psychiatrist's

Do you grab your knitting at the end of a stressful day? If so, notice next time what happens to your inner being as you get absorbed in your knitting. Can you enhance your experience by repeating a mantra or a line of Scripture or poetry?

work is amorphous and never finished," she told me as we sat down together one Saturday at Kiwi. "But working in a yarn shop, I can help people in *concrete* ways, help them to create a product."

The gratification of creating a product, of doing something with a clear end result, is a basic human need, the doctor told me. "In our world, we don't *make* things. So we don't have a sense of fulfillment, and this absence of fulfillment can cause stress. We have too many activities with no end result—like being at the computer all day. Whereas knitting is gratifying: you finish with something tactile and useful."

"Neuroscience," she went on, "has confirmed that making something with your hands settles the busy mind. And knitting is good for other functions of the mind, too: problem solving, math, rhythm, orderliness."

Do her patients knit? "Sometimes it's the right thing for them, yes. Knitting can definitely help with anxiety. And can help break habits like smoking, by keeping your hands busy. Plus it gives them a sense of accomplishment."

Musing later on Brigid's words, I remembered Shakespeare's famous line uttered by Macbeth, who calls on "Sleep that knits up the raveled sleeve of care." Now I want to literalize the knitting metaphor and call on: "Knitting that soothes the troubled spirit to sleep."

Her Mistake Was My Gift

Can making mistakes in your knitting be meditative? *No!* was my definite answer when I first learned to knit. A mistake—a dropped stitch, messing up my decreases, having the wrong number of stitches on a row—would set me into a panic. Gradually, though, I learned how to fix the basic mistakes that every knitter makes. And I learned from more experienced knitters that dealing with one's mistakes is just part of the knitting process.

In fact, figuring out where I went wrong, then figuring out how to fix the mistake: this calls forth all my powers of attention and so is a kind of spiritual discipline. I need to focus intently and patiently on reading my stitches, following the thread, tracing where my work went astray. When I do this, I'm meditating my mistakes.

And sometimes I need to decide whether to leave a mistake as is—when it won't be very visible, or when trying to fix it would likely cause more trouble. The knitters in the discussion at my hometown yarn shop about the spiritual dimensions of knitting offered their experience of making mistakes:

Liza: "If you don't make mistakes, you can't learn to fix them—in knitting and in life."

Liz: "There's a lot of humor among knitters."

Leslie: "It's because we've all been humbled, and humility helps you accept your mistakes, to laugh at them."

I do find it humbling to know that my knitted work will not be perfect. But when are we ever perfect? Jesuit priest James Martin helpfully reminds us in an essay called "God Is Ready," that "your spiritual house does not need to be tidy for God to enter."

Imperfections, untidiness: are they comparable in knitting and in life? Knitters fall into two opposing camps on the question. Characteristic of those who find a continuum between the messes we make in knitting and in life is Susan Gordon Lyden in her book *The Knitting Sutra*. Speaking of her past experiences with knitting, Lyden writes:

> I often made a mistake the moment my mind began to wander. Sometimes I would rip out enough rows to correct the problem, sometimes not, but I began to appreciate these mistakes as small lessons in mindfulness or humility and as expressions of the spirit or soul of the knitting, which seemed to exist apart from me, the knitter. My experience of knitting was enriched the more I knew of spiritual matters, and vice versa. And I found that once I could accept my lack of perfection in both areas with humor and grace, the whole business of knitting, as well as of living, became far more pleasurable to me.

Molly Wolf, editor with Linda Roghaar of the series of knitting-experience anthologies called *KnitLit*, expresses the opposite view in her essay in *KnitLit (too)*. Ripping out one's knitting (called "frogging" by knitters, playing on the sound of *rip-it, rip-it, rip-it*) is one thing, Wolf writes; it's a natural part of the knitting process. "I rip my knitting off the needle without a backward glance." However, she continues:

Unfortunately, while knitting can run backward, unraveling to a particular point, lives can't. We make decisions knowing that they're irreversible, knowing that they may be mistaken, but that they must be made nonetheless. . . . There is no possibility of slipping our lives off the needle and yanking time out to go back to where it went wrong and set it to rights. Not in this life, at least. . . . I wonder sometimes if, after death, God frogs us—holds us firm, undoes the years of pain and wrong and suffering, reknits us together in eternity's womb.

It's a powerful image of the afterlife, I think: this image of God unraveling our wrongs.

To Molly Wolf, only God can reknit our life's errors; to Susan Lydon, we can grow spiritually ("in humor and grace") by learning from our knitting mistakes. But however one views the comparability of the mistakes we make in knitting and in life, most would agree that knitting mistakes can be redemptive. At the Yarn Boutique discussion, Meghan Robinson recounted this experience of unexpected grace:

There was a local Holocaust survivor who knit beautiful suits. She used to knit in the ghetto in Europe. The last time I saw her was in her house. She showed me a sweater and said, "I made it wrong. It doesn't fit me." But she had me try it on—and it fit *me*. She insisted I keep it on even though the weather was very hot that day. She said, "I never usually make these mistakes." But to me it wasn't a mistake. A so-called mistake can fit another person. So it became a gift to me. A sacrament. I haven't worn it yet—but I will. I haven't been quite ready.

Creator and Great Repairer—
I count on you to mend.
When I mess things up, help make them whole.
Please frog my failures, unravel my wrongs.
Help me laugh at my humbling blunders.
Surprise me with your perfect stitches;
May I once in a while find one in my work.

Forgiving

As I've talked with knitters around the country in preparing this book, many have commented that "knitting is very forgiving." They elaborate by explaining that lots of small mistakes don't even show; or that you can nearly always fix a mistake, even after a project is finished; or that when you wash and block your finished work, you can smooth out its unevenness.

This got me to wondering whether there is any spiritual dimension to knitting's forgiveness. As generally used, "forgiving" is a moral term, a moral action. Forgiveness is a core religious value.

The God of the psalms is often extolled for the divine quality of forgiveness. Typical is Psalm 86: "You, O Lord, are good and forgiving, abounding in steadfast love to all who call on you."

Throughout the Gospels, Jesus' foundational action is to forgive our weaknesses, sins, transgressions. His pronouncement of "Go, your sins are forgiven" runs like a refrain through the Gospel of Luke. And Jesus counsels *us* to forgive without limit as well. Famously in Matthew (18:21–22), Jesus instructs Peter to forgive "not seven times, but, I tell you, seventy-seven times." The Lord's Prayer then specifically links God's forgiveness of us with our own forgiveness of others: "forgive us our debts, as we also have forgiven our debtors" (in Matthew's version).

I am reminded that forgiveness as a concept is inseparable from wrongdoing. If we have done no wrong, there is nothing to forgive. Forgiveness says: I know that you have done me wrong, yet I forgive you; or, I see that I have wronged you, and I beg your forgiveness. Forgiveness acknowledges and even embraces our human imperfection.

Approaching knitting in this same spirit can be good for our knitting and for our souls. If I acknowledge from the start of a knitting project that I will surely do something wrong at some point—make small goofs or a major error—then I can be more joyfully relaxed throughout the project. And I can be more accepting of my own imperfection when the inevitable mess-ups appear. Because knitting "is forgiving"—because it allows me to cover over or undo my wrongs—I can forgive myself these wrongs.

These are *not* "moral" wrongs, though. It's important not to confuse knitting's wrongs with those we do to each other. But knitting's forgiving quality can be a metaphor for the forgiveness we try to practice with one another.

During our forty years of marriage, my husband and I have naturally had to practice forgiveness quite often. Forgiveness is inherent to marriage. Over the decades, the images we've used to ask forgiveness were at first borrowed from the technology of the time. In the days of tape recorders, we'd say, "Can I rewind?" Then after computers came in, it was, "Can we delete?" Now that I'm knitting, I like to say, "Can we rip this out and start over?"

God Knows Where It Will Go

I began this book by recounting my first, skeptical encounter with Prayer Shawl knitting. So I want to end by relating two recent personal experiences of the grace that can flow into and from Prayer Shawl groups. The two groups are at nearly opposite ends of the country—in Rochester, New York, and Tucson, Arizona.

I was invited to visit the Prayer Shawl group at Calvary Assembly of God in Rochester during one of their Saturday morning bimonthly gatherings. About a dozen women were there, ranging in age from midtwenties to eighties, chatting happily as they knit away on their projects. They chatted about how to do a particular stitch, about whom their shawl would be for, about how God was working in their own lives through their knitting.

I asked them what drew them to Prayer Shawl ministry, and what it was like for them.

Johanna replied first. "As I'm knitting, I make the shawl so the recipient will be wrapped in the arms of Jesus. I say this in the card I include with the shawl when I give it."

Kathy explained to me that she's a new knitter. "God drew me to this ministry, so I had to learn to knit . . . everyone here taught me." And who, I inquired, would receive the shawl she was at that moment working on? Kathy didn't miss a stitch as she answered: "I ask the Holy Spirit to guide me in prayer for who should receive the shawl. When I start, I don't know whom it's for."

This became a motif in their conversation: the trust that God would find the right recipient for one's knitted work. Karen summed up the group's consensus: "We can pray while knitting because God knows where it will go."

The Prayer Shawl group at Saguaro Canyon Evangelical Free Church in Tucson knows exactly where their shawls will go, in a sense. They don't know precisely which person will receive which shawl. But all year they are knitting shawls for their church's Blue Christmas service, held annually on December 21—because this is the longest night of the year. The entire community is welcomed to the Blue Christmas service, especially anyone who "feels blue" at Christmas time because of a loss or other suffering. And anyone needing hope and prayers is wrapped in a shawl, their gift to take home, symbolic of God's comforting embrace.

Every shawl is unique, since each knitter or crocheter uses her own pattern. The one rule is that the shawls be made in some variant of shades of blue.

"As you're working on your shawl," the group's volunteer coordinator, Debbie Stertz, told me, "it's a long process, so you can't help but knit into your work your prayers and hopes for whoever might eventually receive it."

I learned about the Blue Christmas service while I was writing this book, so naturally I was eager to attend. As I walked into the church that evening of December 21, I went right over to the piles of shawls (including lap robes for men) on a table at the back of the sanctuary. Thirty in all—each one indeed different in design and in shades of blue. But all richly thick with warm, cozy, chunky yarn.

Debbie's daughter, Chelsea, led the worship for that year's Blue Christmas. She also led the group of four young adult musicians who played throughout the service. Rows of chairs for attendees were arranged in an arc around a microphone and a table of candles. Some candles were lit; others were dark. After singing opening songs about life's burdens and God's healing love, Chelsea invited those present to come to the microphone, tell why they were there, and light a candle symbolizing God's light shining in our darkness.

Many of the people who came forward lit a candle for someone else: for a colleague whose wife had suddenly died last month; for a sister with breast cancer; for a friend confined to a wheelchair. A few told their own stories, their own sorrows and needs and hopes. A young man joyfully explained how he and his wife were to become foster parents on Christmas Day, taking into their lives two children who had suffered great abuse; he lit a candle for each of them.

Without in the least intending to—I'd come to the service as an observer, to write about it for this book—I found myself walking to

the microphone. I spoke about the leukemia I'd been diagnosed with several years ago, about how the unlit candles on the table were like the dark and scared part of me, the part afraid that God might not always be there for whatever the future would bring; and I lit a candle in prayer that God's light would shine into my whole being, so that I might trust more fully that God would lead me through this illness.

A few other people spoke and lit candles. Chelsea led some songs and then announced that members of the congregation were available to join anyone who needed special prayers. "You will be given a hand-knit shawl, and as you are wrapped in the shawl, be wrapped in love and be blessed," she ended. Several hands went up; people carrying shawls approached them; small groups of prayer quietly formed. I sat alone in the peace of it all. Then a young couple sitting a few empty seats away from me spontaneously slid closer and asked if I'd like them to pray for me. I nodded a grateful yes. Sitting on either side of me, they each took one of my hands, and the young man prayed for our deep trust that God embraces our lives and for my peace during the course of the leukemia. Then the young woman got up, went to the table of shawls, and brought one to me.

So I went home that evening gifted with a prayer shawl, feeling blessed by this couple, blessed by Chelsea's prayerful leading of worship and song throughout the service, and—yes—blessed by the love knit into every stitch of my new shawl.

PATTERNING YOUR PRAYER
Feather Lace Washcloth
by Lynn Davis

Patterns for prayer shawls are easily available online, so instead we offer you this washcloth designed by the owner of Tucson's Kiwi Knitting Company. It makes a delightful gift: everyone can use a washcloth, for kitchen or bath, and the lacy pattern has a cheery, lighthearted look.

Knitting this pattern, you can practice two of the kinds of meditation discussed in this book. The even-numbered rows don't demand attention and so invite the mind into a mantra or prayer for whoever will receive this gift. The decreases and yarn-overs of the odd-numbered rows require attention, drawing the mind away from any troubles.

K2tog = Knit 2 stitches together.

K2togtbl = Knit 2 stitches together through back loop.

YO = yarn over (wrap yarn once around right needle counter-clockwise).

Sl1-K2tog-PSSO = slip next stitch purlwise; knit next 2 stitches together; pass the slipped stitch over the K2tog stitch and off the needle.

Gauge: 18 stitches = 4".

Yarn: Lynn used one ball of Debbie Bliss "Eco" cotton yarn. You can use 50 grams of any 100 percent cotton yarn at Aran (worsted) weight. The yarn for a washcloth must be 100 percent cotton to hold water well.

Needles: US8 or other size to obtain gauge.

Instructions:

Cast on 44 stitches.

Work 6 rows of garter stitch (that is, knitting each row).

Begin Feather Lace pattern:

Row 1: K4, *YO, K2togtbl, K1, K2tog, YO, K1, repeat from * 5 more times, K4.

All even-numbered Rows 2–8: K4, Purl36, K4.

Row 3: K4, *YO, K1, Sl1-K2tog-PSSO, K1, YO, K1, repeat from * 5 more times, K4.

Row 5: K4, *K2tog, YO, K1, YO, K2togtbl, K1, repeat from * 5 more times, K4.

Row 7: K3, K2tog, *K1, YO, K1, YO, K1, Sl1-K2tog-PSSO, repeat from * to last 9 stitches, K1, YO, K1, YO, K1, K2togtbl, K4.

Repeat Rows 1–8 5 more times.

Work Rows 1–7 once more.

Work 6 rows of garter stitch.

Bind off all stitches.

Acknowledgments

First, my thanks to the many people who shared with me their knitting experiences and gave me permission to use their words in this book. Two people from the newer generation of knitters were gracious enough to read my manuscript while it was in process. My gratitude to Amanda Rayburn and Meghan Robinson for their thoughtful readings and helpful comments. Huge thanks as well to the designers who created the patterns at the end of each chapter of the book: Sviatlana Harnizonava, Valerie McPherson, Tina Turner, Marilyn Schubert, and Lynn Davis.

Thanks to everyone at Paraclete Press for believing in this book and for working with conscientious joy to produce it. Special thanks to my editor, Maura Shaw, who has been a delight to work with. She was the perfect editor for this project: as a knitter herself, she could enter fully into both the spirit and the details of the book, offering helpful suggestions and insights throughout.

Thanks to the knitters in my family for their support and inspiration: my sister Amy, who from the start brainstormed ideas for the book with me; my husband, George, supportive of all my projects but of this one in a special way, since he shares my love of knitting; and granddaughters Jordan and Phoebe, without whom I might never have become a knitter.

Grateful acknowledgment is made to the following writers and publishers for granting permission to reprint portions of these works:

Bonn, Sally, lines from "Catapult, Cull, Collide & Commune," in *Orange* (Rochester, NY: 2009). Reprinted with permission of the poet.

Bristow, Janet, "Good God!" prayer. Reprinted with permission of shawlministry.com.

Cairns, Scott, lines from "Evening Prayer," *Compass of Affection* (Paraclete Press, 2006). Reprinted with permission of Paraclete Press.

Chase, Joelle, lines from "Knitting," posted to blog alivening.blogspot.com in December 2008. Reprinted with permission of the poet.

Cline, Willa, lines from "I Would Knit You Socks," posted at willa.com/weblog/2005/04/i-would-knit-you-socks.htm. Reprinted with permission of the poet.

Henager, Pamela, from July 31, 2006, post "The Japanese Sweater as Metaphor" on her blog pamsknitting.blogspot.com. Reprinted with permission of the author.

Kownacki, Mary Lou, lines from *Between Two Souls* (Grand Rapids: Eerdmans, 2004). Reprinted with permission of the poet.

Murtha, Cathleen O'Meara, "As we gather in community" prayer. Reprinted with permission of shawlministry.com.

Reuter, Melanie C., from "Knitting as a Spiritual Journey," May 27, 2008, post at blog HandsToSoul.wordpress.com. Reprinted with permission of the author.

Shaw, Luci, journal entry reprinted in *Breath for the Bones: Art, Imagination, and Spirit* (Nashville: Thomas Nelson, 2007). Reprinted with permission of Luci Shaw and Thomas Nelson Publishers.

Walker, Jeanne Murray, lines from "Sister Storm," *Image* 53 (Spring 2007). Reprinted with permission of the poet and *Image*.

Notes

Chapter One—Knit One, Purl a Prayer

Tara Jon Manning, *Mindful Knitting* (Boston: Tuttle Publishing, 2004), 4.

All quotations from the Qur'an are from Abdullah Yusuf Ali, *The Meanings of the Holy Qur'an: English Translation with Foot Notes* (New Delhi: Islamic Book Service, 2001).

The quotations from Anthony Bloom, *Beginning to Pray* (Mahwah, NJ: Paulist Press, 1907) are from pages 92–94.

Mother Theodora is quoted in Henry L. Carrigan, Jr., ed., *Eternal Wisdom from the Desert* (Brewster, MA: Paraclete Press, 2001), 96.

Bishop Theophan is quoted in Timothy Ware, ed., *The Art of Prayer* (London: Faber and Faber, 1966), 83.

Cathleen O'Meara Murtha's prayer is at www.shawlministry.com.

Chapter Two—Knit One, Purl a Passage

Cassian's words about our feelings becoming our teachers are from his *Conference* 10.11.6, quoted in Columba Stewart, *Cassian the Monk* (New York: Oxford University Press, 1998), 112.

Patrick J. Willson's quotation is from "Reflections on the Lectionary," *The Christian Century* (August 24, 2010), 21.

The quotation from *The Bhagavad Gita* is Juan Mascaro's translation (New York: Penguin Books, 1962), 6:20–27.

Sarah Klassen's poem "The Potter" appears in *Image* 62 (Summer 2009), 61.

Scott Cairns's poem "Evening Prayer" appears in *Compass of Affection* (Brewster, MA: Paraclete Press, 2006), 159.

The passages quoted from Mary Lou Kownacki's poetic conversation with Ryokan in *Between Two Souls* (Grand Rapids: Eerdmans, 2004) are on pages 52–53.

Willa Cline's poem is at willa.com/weblog/2005/04/i-would-knit-you-socks.htm.

Joelle's poem is at alivening.blogspot.com/2008/12/knitting.html.

Sally Bittner Bonn's "Catapult, Cull, Collide & Commune" is in her collection *Orange* (Rochester, NY: 2009), 5.

Jeanne Murray Walker's poem "Sister Storm" appears in *Image* 53 (Spring 2007), 110.

Chapter Three—Knit One, Purl a Community

The quotation from *The Rural Life of England* can be found in Richard Rutt, *A History of Hand Knitting* (Loveland, CO: Interweave Press, 1987), 120.

Molly Oliver's words are from a personal interview, April 13, 2010.

The charity knitting groups listed in *Interweave Knits* are at interweaveknits.com/community/charities.asp.

The prayer from First Presbyterian Church of Normal, Illinois, "Gracious God, we give thanks . . ." is at firstpresnormal.org/life/knitting. htm. Retrieved August, 2009.

The quotation by Sidney is from *The Countesse of Pembroke's Arcadia*, facsimile edition (London: Cambridge University Press, 1965), 13. I have modernized the spelling.

Thanks to Jane Davis for calling my attention to the Lorenzetti painting.

The quotation by Julian of Norwich is in the translation of Fr. John-Julian, OJN, *The Complete Julian of Norwich* (Brewster, MA: Paraclete Press, 2009), 261. Thanks to Amy Frykholm for pointing me to this passage and for presenting the major role of sheep, the wool trade, and knitting in fourteenth-century Norwich in her *Julian of Norwich: A Contemplative Biography* (Brewster, MA: Paraclete Press, 2010).

Chapter Four—Knit One, Purl a Pattern

The epigraph by Denise Frame Harlan is from her "Spinning a Yarn: or Giving It a Whirl," February 2007, at catapultmagazine.com/with-my-own-two-hands/article/spinning-a-yarn.

Pam Henager's post on the Japanese sweater pattern is at pamsknitting.blogspot.com/2006/07/japanese-sweater-as-metaphor.html.

Composer James MacMillan's comment about active listening is from his article "Why Sacred Music Endures" in *Image* 63 (Fall 2009): 85.

The quotations from Deborah Bergman, *The Knitting Goddess* (New York: Hyperion, 2000) are on pages 6–8.

Luci Shaw's remark about seeing pictures in our heads is from her book *Breath for the Bones: Art, Imagination, and Spirit* (Nashville: Thomas Nelson, 2007), 18.

Denise Frame Harlan's reflections about how "you can make things yourself" were written in February 2007 at catapultmagazine.com/with-my-own-two-hands/article/spinning-a-yarn.

Shaw's journal entry was later printed in her *Breath for the Bones*, 74–75.

Chapter Five—Knit One, Purl the Pain

The epigraph by Elizabeth Zimmermann is from her *Knitting Without Tears* (New York: Simon & Schuster, 1971), 2.

Betsy Greer's report on the scientific evidence for knitting's ability to reduce pain can be found in her *Knitting for Good* (Boston: Trumpeter Books, 2008), 46–47.

M. Craig Barnes' quote from the nursing home resident is in his article "Holy Ground," *The Christian Century* (May 19, 2009), 11.

Naomi Shihab Nye's poem "Breaking My Favorite Bowl" appears in her collection *Words Under the Words* (Portland, OR: Eighth Mountain Press, 1995), 120.

Kathryn Gunn's report of her KIPping journey appears at knittinguniverse.com/xrx/community/KnitU_Detail.php?DigestNumber=1666. Retrieved July, 2010.

Susan Mark Landis's reflections on knitting as a Christian Peacemaker Team member are at peace.mennolink.org/cgi-bin/m.pl?a=197, May 17, 2005.

Chapter Six—Knit Two, Purl a Prayer

Chuang Tzu's tale of the woodcarver is from a translation by Thomas Merton in *The Way of Chuang Tzu* (New York: New Directions, 1965), 110.

Dyana Herron's reflection on creating with our hands is in her *Good Letters* post, November 25, 2009, at imagejournal.org.

The quotations from Kat Welsh's article "Knitting Yourself Together" are at knitty.com/ISSUEsummer03/FEATknittingyourself.html.

James Martin's remark that "your spiritual house does not need to be tidy for God to enter" is in his article "God Is Ready," *America* (March 8, 2010), 18.

The quotation from Susan Gordon Lyden, *The Knitting Sutra* (New York: HarperCollins, 1997) is on page 104.

Molly Wolf's speculation that "God frogs us" is from Linda Roghaar and Molly Wolf, eds., *KnitLit (too)* (New York: Three Rivers Press, 2004), 181–83.

About Paraclete Press

Who We Are

Paraclete Press is a publisher of books, recordings, and DVDs on Christian spirituality. Our publishing represents a full expression of Christian belief and practice—from Catholic to Evangelical, from Protestant to Orthodox.

We are the publishing arm of the Community of Jesus, an ecumenical monastic community in the Benedictine tradition. As such, we are uniquely positioned in the marketplace without connection to a large corporation and with informal relationships to many branches and denominations of faith.

What We Are Doing

Books

Paraclete publishes books that show the richness and depth of what it means to be Christian. Although Benedictine spirituality is at the heart of all that we do, we publish books that reflect the Christian experience across many cultures, time periods, and houses of worship. We publish books that nourish the vibrant life of the church and its people—books about spiritual practice, formation, history, ideas, and customs.

We have several different series, including the best-selling Paraclete Essentials, and Paraclete Giants series of classic texts in contemporary English; A Voice from the Monastery—men and women monastics writing about living a spiritual life today; award-winning literary faith fiction and poetry; and the Active Prayer Series that brings creativity and liveliness to any life of prayer.

Recordings

From Gregorian chant to contemporary American choral works, our music recordings celebrate sacred choral music through the centuries. Paraclete distributes the recordings of the internationally acclaimed choir Gloriæ Dei Cantores, praised for their "rapt and fathomless spiritual intensity" by *American Record Guide,* and the Gloriæ Dei Cantores Schola, which specializes in the study and performance of Gregorian chant. Paraclete is also the exclusive North American distributor of the recordings of the Monastic Choir of St. Peter's Abbey in Solesmes, France, long considered to be a leading authority on Gregorian chant.

DVDs

Our DVDs offer spiritual help, healing, and biblical guidance for life issues: grief and loss, marriage, forgiveness, anger management, facing death, and spiritual formation.

Learn more about us at our website:
www.paracletepress.com, or call us toll-free at 1-800-451-5006.

Also in the Active Prayer series

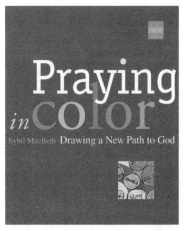

Praying in Color Drawing a New Path to God
Sybil MacBeth

If you are word-weary, stillness-challenged, easily distracted, or just in need of a new way to pray, give "praying in color" a try. Sybil MacBeth introduces a simple, creative, joy-filled prayer practice.

"Just as Julia Cameron in *The Artist's Way* showed the hardened Harvard businessman he had a creative artist lurking within, MacBeth makes it astonishingly clear that anyone with a box of colors and some paper can have a conversation with God. Readers of all ages, experience, and religions will find this a fresh, invigorating, and even exhilarating way to spend time with themselves and their Creator."—*Publishers Weekly*

ISBN: 978-1-55725-512-9 | $16.95 Paperback

————

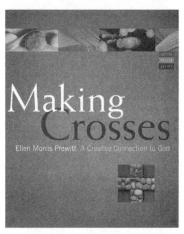

Making Crosses A Creative Connection to God
Ellen Morris Prewitt

The practice of making a cross takes you beyond analytic thinking, and offers a way of prayer where understanding comes from doing. Working with the most complex symbol of Christianity—the cross—we learn to cocreate with God in concrete and tangible ways.

ISBN: 978-1-55725-628-7 | $16.99 Paperback

————

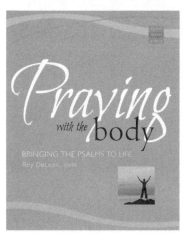

Praying with the Body Bringing the Psalms to Life
Roy DeLeon

While most books about prayer are meant to be read, this one is an invitation to move in prayer by expressing the Psalms with motion. Benedictine oblate Roy DeLeon guides you with helpful drawings, Scripture texts, and explanations.

ISBN: 978-1-55725-589-1 | $17.99 Paperback

Available from most booksellers or through Paraclete Press;
www.paracletepress.com; 1-800-451-5006. Try your local bookstore first.